FEARLESS INTERVIEWING

How to Win the Job by Communicating with Confidence

Marky Stein

McGraw-Hill

New York   Chicago   San Francisco
Lisbon   London   Madrid   Mexico City
Milan   New Delhi   San Juan   Seoul
Singapore   Sydney   Toronto

5 6 7 8 9 0   AGM/AGM   0 9 8 7 6 5 4

ISBN 0-07-140884-3

McGraw-Hill books are available at special quantity discounts to use as premiums and sales promotions, or for use in corporate training programs. For more information, please write to the Director of Special Sales, Professional Publishing, McGraw-Hill, Two Penn Plaza, New York, NY 10121-2298. Or contact your local bookstore.

Library of Congress Cataloging-in-Publication Data

Stein, Marky.
   Fearless interviewing : how to win the job by communicating
   with confidence / by Marky Stein.
      p. cm.
   ISBN 0-07-140884-3 (acid-free)
   1. Employment interviewing. I. Title.
HF5549.5.I6 S728 2003
658.3'1124—dc21

                                              2002015420

CONTENTS

Contents

Contents

ACKNOWLEDGMENTS

To my first career counselor, Astrid Berg, who told me, "If it's in your heart, do it."

To Jack Stein, Rusty Stein, Jill Stein, Melissa Greer, Krishna Roman, and Saundra Ridel, whose love and gentle guidance have shown me that for every challenge, there is a spiritual solution.

Special thanks to Wilma Marcus, Steven Beasley, Kate Smith, Maggie Smith, Michael Mersman, Jack Chapman, Debbie Featherston, Carolyn Clark, Bill Shipley, and Mark Guterman for helping me discover a great well of ideas, courage, and creativity, and, most of all, the resolve to express them.

Finally, my deepest gratitude to my editor, Michelle Howry, for her unwavering faith in me and my work.

Thank you.

Marky Stein

One can never consent to creep when one feels an impulse to soar.

—Helen Keller

Why Are Interviews So Scary?

> *It takes courage to live a life, any life.*
>
> —Erica Jong

Have you ever felt jittery before an interview? Nervous or even terrified? Have you ever wished you had answered a question differently or negotiated your salary more skillfully? Do you panic when you imagine the possibility of "failure"? Do you just want to make sure you get it right the first time?

Let's face it. Interviews are not like normal conversations. Being interviewed can be scary, even for ordinarily outgoing people. When you're sitting in the hot seat, the interviewer is an authority figure, and he or she has all or most of the power in the interview.

Guess what? Studies show that more than 60 percent of interviewers have never been trained in the task of interviewing. Most of these managers report that they feel "nervous, anxious, confused, stressed" and even "incompetent" when taking on the responsibility of conducting a job interview.

Now that you're reading *Fearless Interviewing*, take another look at who's being trained and who's not!

> *It's likely that you're actually going to be more prepared for the meeting than the interviewer.*

Think again. Now who holds the power? By the end of this book, you'll find that you too have control over what goes on at the interview, especially when you learn to harness your fear into excitement, energy, and enthusiasm. To make this transformation you'll need to learn the techniques of fearless interviewing.

Here's how one of my clients, Christine, used fearless interviewing to turn her timidity into power.

Christine's Story

Christine came to see me for some career coaching after a series of failed interviews. She told me that she had interviewed at several high-profile financial firms for a position as a financial analyst. She had a B.A. in accounting and a master's in business administration, plus eight years' experience as a senior accountant and financial analyst for a midsized company in Montana.

From my evaluation of the résumé she sent me, neither her qualifications nor her education were the problem.

When Christine came to my office for an appointment, she told me that she had been out of work for several months and added emphatically that interviewing had been "torture" for her. She said that she felt timid at the interviews she had gone to and that she felt intensely uncomfortable about being asked questions that required her to call attention to herself and her skills.

Though perfectly well qualified for just about any financial analyst position, Christine suffered from what is sometimes known in psychology as the *imposter syndrome*. The imposter syndrome presents itself as the feeling that, even though we have accomplished something, we somehow feel that we don't deserve the recognition or prestige that goes with it.

According to Christine, "I've never had a problem talking about a friend's accomplishments, but when it comes to my own, I find it embarrassing." She reports, "I'm afraid that others will think I'm arrogant. I feel that if I boast about myself at an interview, the company might hire me and then find out I can't do the job at all."

At first, as Christine learned the techniques of fearless interviewing, she told me that she felt uncomfortable relating her strengths in such a straightforward manner. "It feels like bragging," she said. But as we worked together to reframe her notion of "bragging" into one of simply "reporting the facts," she began to relax and handle questions about herself more easily.

When Christine built her skills arsenal and constructed her Q statements (as you'll do in Chapters 2 and 3, she realized that her strengths were not just fabrications; they were real. Furthermore, they could be *proven* by citing examples of what she had actually done in the real world!

> **Her accomplishments, she soon learned,
> were not exaggerations at all; they were simply
> statements of facts.**

Christine's next interview was with a Fortune 500 financial organization for a job as a financial analyst. I heard from her about 2 weeks after the interview took place. She sent me a greeting card with the face of a sad, cute little puppy on the front of it. The inside of the card said, "Before, I felt like a scared puppy; now I feel like a lion! Thank you for helping me land the job!"

Just like Christine, many of us shy away from "tooting our own horns."

> *But that's just what an interview is for. It's your opportunity to tell an employer what you've accomplished in the past and how you'll help them in the future.*

When Christine was able to interview successfully for the financial analyst position, nothing new or magical was added to her personality. She simply picked up the tools that we're going to discuss in the coming chapters.

Most important, she learned to let the employer understand, in clear and specific terms, that she *could* and *would* make a significant contribution to that firm.

> *This is the key to fearless interviewing: knowing your strengths, being able to provide concrete examples of those strengths, thereby building the lasting confidence to present yourself and your skills in the best possible light.*

In the next several chapters, you'll learn the following:

- What interviewers are *really* looking for
- How to charm your way into the interviewer's heart in the first 20 seconds of the interview
- How to express your strengths and skills with power and laserlike precision
- How to handle even the most difficult questions
- How to use body language in your favor

- How to leverage multiple job offers
- The most important questions to ask the employer
- How to be a master at negotiating your salary

My Story

In the next chapter, we'll take a look at some of the fears you too are going to leave behind, but before we explore the rest of the techniques I've told you about, I'd like to tell you a little bit about how I became a career coach and how I came to write this book.

I became a career coach in 1989 for many reasons, but there's only one reason that really counts. I simply *love* talking to people about their work! Even before I was a counselor, I had a sort of innate sense that every person has a certain career destiny. I was absolutely fascinated by people's career choices—how they started doing what they were doing, if they liked their work, and especially if they had a secret dream about what they'd really like to be doing. For some reason it seemed just as natural to me to talk about people's careers as it was to talk about their pets, their gardens, or a movie they had seen.

But even though talking about careers seemed to come naturally to me, becoming a career counselor wasn't nearly as easy as that. I faced many of the same feelings of rejection and frustration as other people sometimes feel in interviews. Shortly before I took up career coaching as a profession, I decided to ask a few professional career counselors whether they thought I was suited to the occupation, what I could expect from being a career counselor, and what the job prospects were like. All 10 of the people I talked to said I would "never make it" without a master's degree in counseling or education. I didn't have one, and I didn't plan to get one soon.

One said: "None of the agencies are hiring—the economy's too soft. There's a waiting list of over a thousand people from all over the world trying to get the one job at the local community college." (Sound familiar?)

Still another professional warned: "I'd hate to see you waste your time trying to build a career coaching business in this town. It's too small, and I've never known any counselor to succeed at it."

After 10 of those less-than-inspiring "pep talks," I was ready to move out of town—and get a job doing just about anything else *except* career counseling! But I didn't. Somehow their warnings posed a challenge for me. I had broken into other difficult fields when everyone said it was impossible. I knew I could do it again.

I immediately started offering free talks to all sorts of organizations on goal setting, self-esteem, and résumé writing. I attended some professional seminars and conferences on career development. I read every single book I could get my hands on about careers and jobs, and I took some graduate courses in career development and counseling.

Within 6 months of deciding to become a career counselor, I had appointments booked for 2 months with a waiting list!

I worked with clients in industries as diverse as publishing, biotechnology, semiconductors, sales, the arts, entertainment, telecommunications, medicine, law, computers, defense, Web design, engineering, hospitality, foods, and even wine making. I taught workshops and worked individually with people in all walks of life—students and executives and entry-level employees and Ph.D.s.

One day, in one of my classes, a woman exclaimed, "You know, you should write a book!" I liked the idea, mostly because it represented another challenge and because I realized that indeed, I could keep teaching job seeking skills to 10 or 20 people at a time, or I could reach thousands of people all at once!

I wrote the first chapter of the book you're reading right now and submitted it to the top literary agent in San Francisco. I was sure he would love my idea and see it as an instant success.

Two weeks later, I got a generic rejection letter, without even a real signature. When I called and asked him about it, the editor said, "Good title, but who would read it? I'm sorry, we can't represent your book."

I was crushed; but I refused to let the rejection stop me. I was convinced that I had a valuable message for job seekers, one with important tools that would ensure their success. After a few more disappointments from other literary agents, I decided to take matters into my own hands and publish the book myself.

Sure I went into debt. Sure I was scared. But soon—after I'd flown all over the country giving Fearless Interviewing seminars, appeared on radio and TV, and been written about in magazines and newspapers—my efforts paid off.

One morning while I was going through my usual routine, I picked up the phone, and it was the beautiful voice of a New York editor! She told me that she had seen an article written by me, and that she was interested in my book. I was so stunned after she said "hello" and introduced herself that I said, "Excuse me. Would you hold on for just a moment? I've got to find my body and then get back into it."

The motto? Perseverance. Maybe interviews 1, 2, or even 3 didn't go as well as you liked. But with the ammunition in this book, we'll turn numbers 4, 5, and 6 into offers. I *know* you can do it!

CHAPTER ONE

An Assault against Anxiety

The door of opportunity won't open unless you do some pushing.

—Anonymous

Tim was the head of a lighting crew for a local television news station in Salt Lake City, Utah. After 4 years of working on the crew and finally becoming the chief lighting designer, he figured he had paid his dues and was ready to move to Los Angeles to get a job in the film industry.

With no binding family ties or other obligations, he packed up his pickup truck and headed for Hollywood. It was 4 months before he landed his first interview, a meeting with the director of photography for a network movie-of-the-week. He was willing to start at the bottom, but unfortunately, the interview failed to yield the chance to do even *that*.

"It was like an interrogation," he protested when he called me. "I never expected to have to tell my life story just to get a job on a movie! Their questions were impossible. I'm not a brain surgeon."

"I don't know what happened," he reflected. "When they asked those questions about my weaknesses and my failures, my mouth went dry, and it was like my jaw couldn't move. I just sat there and totally froze! They must have thought I was a moron! I walked out of there shaking inside, feeling like I was a total idiot. There's *no way* I'm ever going to go through anything like that again!"

You're certainly not alone if you have some negative feelings about interviewing. Most people consider interviews to be somewhere between mildly unpleasant and absolutely terrifying. This book will give you specific strategies for conquering that anxiety and quieting those negative voices.

The Most Common Interview Fears

The 11 most common fears that people have voiced to me about interviewing are contained in the following checklist. Check the box next to any of these fears you have right now. Be sure to use a pencil! You're going to go back over this list at the end of reading this book, and I can safely predict that many of the fears you have now will most certainly have been "erased" by then.

☐ *I fear they will ask me a question I don't know the answer to.* Chapters 2 through 5, plus the sample interviews at the end of the book, will leave you with no doubt about how to strategically answer any of the four types of interview questions.

☐ *I'm afraid I'll sound like I'm bragging.* Many of us learned in childhood or later that "blowing your own horn" is a sign of being on an ego trip. But providing information about the nature of work you have done is not doing that. In Chapter 3, you'll see the difference between bragging and simply stating the facts.

☐ *Do I have to say I was fired from my last job? Can they find out?* There are laws that protect you from potential employers' prying into your past in ways that are inappropriate. We'll discuss those laws as well as how best to deal with questions that pertain to past employment situations.

☐ *Everyone says I am under/overqualified. What should I do?* Usually the employer who says he or she is worried about either of these issues actually has a hidden agenda. We'll find out exactly how to address and defuse that agenda in Chapter 5 when we talk about "questions behind questions."

☐ *Do I have to submit to drug testing, credit checks, or personality tests?* Drug testing, credit checks, and personality tests are a reality of today's workplace and hard to avoid. You may simply decide you don't want to work at a place with such restrictive entrance procedures.

☐ *What should I do if an interviewer asks me an intrusive or illegal question?* Some topics, such as disabilities, marital status, or sexual orientation, are off-limits during an interview. We'll talk about how to avoid these incriminating and illegal questions.

☐ *I don't know what to do with my hands during an interview.* This is a very common worry. Once you know the one most potent secret of nonverbal behavior in an interview, you'll find your hands will just fall into place, and you won't even have to think about them!

☐ *I fear I will just "freeze up" in the interview.* You'll learn the technique of "stalling and accessing," which is a convincing and comfortable way out of this one. It will seem very natural, once you learn it.

☐ *I had to answer technical questions. They were easy, and I knew I had answered them right. The interviewer said I answered them wrong. What do I do in a situation like that?* Sound familiar? If you're an engineer or scientist, you've very likely faced this type of scenario. It can be unnerving! We'll teach you how to answer the question and keep your cool in Chapter 5, in the section on "stress questions."

☐ *Do I have to reveal how much money I made at my last job? How and when should I bring up the issue of salary?* We'll discuss every nuance of salary negotiations in Chapter 7. Not only will you be able to handle salary discussions, you'll be able to master them.

☐ *How do I explain that I was laid off?* There's a simple way to phrase information about a layoff that leaves you blameless and dignified. It's contained in Chapter 5.

In addition to helping you float with ease in the shark-infested waters of these common fears, the fearless interviewing approach will do for you what most other books on the subject fail to do, and that is to focus on mastering four categories of questions and answers. Being prepared this way will enable you to answer questions with ease and authority.

Strategy versus Memorization

Most books on interviewing treat each question as a separate entity. For example, they may suggest 100 answers to the most common interview questions, with the expectation that you will remember whichever ones seem relevant when the time comes. That's fine if you have an encyclopedic memory, but a strategy is even better. Fearless interviewing is an entirely new approach to the process of interviewing that uses *strategy* instead of memory.

You won't be memorizing endless pages of interview questions, and I won't be telling you the exact words to say. You won't have to memorize anything that doesn't come naturally to you. Instead, we'll be learning strategies—basic principles that leave you free to express yourself in the most comfortable way possible.

41m

You'll learn how to divide questions into four major categories and develop an overall plan for answering each type of question. For example, the questions "What are your strengths?" and "What are your weaknesses?" actually belong to two entirely different categories. The first is what I call a straightforward question, and the second is what I call a stress question. Each requires a different, almost opposite, strategy to answer successfully. You'll learn the most advantageous approach for each of these questions, and many more, in the following pages!

> **With fearless interviewing techniques, you'll have to keep track of only four categories instead of hundreds of questions.**

Interviewing Can Be Fun!

As you read this book, I hope that you'll go through the process of "reframing" what an interview means to you. Reframing is the process of transforming how you perceive a situation so that you can look at it in a different, usually better, way. By gaining confidence in your interviewing skills, you'll cease to see the interview as some sort of uncomfortable interrogation, and you'll begin to see it as an incredible opportunity for learning, pleasure, and even fun.

Once you do an inventory of your skills (which we will do in the next chapter), you will see that the interview is merely a forum for you to enjoy talking about what you do best and love doing most. Imagine that! A job interview that's fun!

Learning how to interview fearlessly is like learning how to dance. There are some basic steps to master. At first you learn and practice each step slowly, but before long you find yourself gliding across the floor. You've picked up the right book to help you learn those steps, and with just a little bit of practice, you'll be flying. Let's go for it!

CHAPTER TWO

Building Your Skills Arsenal

> *The road to happiness lies in two simple principles: Find what it is that interests you and that you can do well, and put your whole soul into it—every bit of energy and ambition and natural ability that you have.*
>
> —John D. Rockefeller

Marie first telephoned me on a Wednesday sounding upset and confused. "I've blown the seventh interview in 2 months. I think I need an interview coach."

"I just can't understand it," she continued. "I had my résumé done professionally. You should see it. It can't have to do with my appearance. Every time before I go to an interview, I get my hair done, I have a manicure, and I always wear my best suits. I really don't know what to think. It makes me wonder if I'm in the wrong profession! If another person with less experience gets the job instead of me again, I'm literally going to scream!"

Marie faxed me her résumé the day before our appointment together. On paper, she looked terrific. It was clear from her résumé that she had a 10-year background in sales, had managed over 75 people, and had handled some formidable accounts of up to several million dollars each. Given the right presentation at an interview, Marie could probably have her pick of a number of sales positions in the tech industry.

She came for her coaching appointment on a Friday. In the first few seconds, it was clear to me that she had excellent social skills. Her greeting was professional, and she had a winning smile and a firm businesslike handshake. She looked me straight in the eye and stood tall, appearing to have a lot of confidence. She was dressed and accessorized impeccably. There certainly was nothing *not* to like about her. It was clear to me from the outset that first impressions were not her problem.

Marie and I decided that we would do a mock interview where I would play the interviewer and she would play herself. The first question I asked her is probably the most common first question asked in any interview: "Tell me about yourself." I followed with some other common questions like, "Tell me about your skills," and "What is your greatest strength?"

> **What evidence did I have that she was, in fact, a top performer? How did she plan to apply her skills to make profits for my company?**

Marie's answers to my questions, though technically correct, were fraught with generalities and gave only a vague impression of what she actually could offer as a marketing director. Had I been an employer, I might have had questions and doubts as to whether she could really perform as well as she said she could. How, specifically, could she prove her skills?

- For example, what did she mean when she said she was "extremely experienced"?
  ✓ Did she mean 2 years' experience? 5 years'? Perhaps 20?
- And she says she has an "exceptional record of service."
  ✓ What exactly is it that made her service exceptional?
  ✓ Did she mean she had exceeded her quotas?
  ✓ Did she mean she had handled accounts with an unusually high monetary value?
- What about her comment that she has "an outstanding sense of the needs of the marketplace"?
  ✓ Was she adept at market research?
  ✓ Could she give me a specific example of being able to understand the needs of a customer?

I was not surprised when she said that her greatest strength was good communication skills. Most of us, in fact, believe that we have good communication skills. The challenge is that, in an interview, you have to be able to prove it.

  ✓ Could she tell me about some presentations she had made that won accounts?
  ✓ Had she engaged in negotiations that resulted in the favor of her company? When? With whom? How much money was involved?
  ✓ Perhaps she meant she was good at resolving conflicts through communication.

It was hard to know exactly what Marie meant since she didn't really have the specific data to back up her assertions. This kind of crucial data is exactly the kind of ammunition we'll be gathering in the next two chapters. You don't have to make the same mistakes that Marie made. You will know your skills and exactly how they can make a positive impact on whatever organization you're applying to. Unlike Marie you *won't* do the following:

- Think your résumé will speak *for* you.
- Speak in generalities and expect the interviewer to "connect the dots" for you.

No wonder. Marie kept getting turned down for jobs in spite of her friendly and businesslike demeanor. Employers want proof of your abilities! The reality is that, before an employer pays Marie over $100,000 per year to act as his or her sales director, the employer will want to have some specific examples of where and how Marie had used those skills to produce positive results for another company. Marie cannot expect her résumé to "do the talking" for her. Instead, she has to learn to clearly and succinctly verbalize those results.

> *In the next two chapters you will learn how you can easily avoid the pitfall of sounding too vague simply by knowing your skills and knowing how to communicate them with confidence.*
> *Let's move on to the good stuff!*

Assessing Your Skills

Taking an inventory of your skills is the beginning of being successful in any job interview. Ninety percent of employers say that the primary reason they do not hire a candidate is because the interviewee *could not clearly state his or her skills*. Read that last sentence again. That doesn't mean they didn't *have* the skills necessary to do the job. It means that they could not verbally *state* those skills in a convincing way.

When you've finished the exercises in the next two chapters, you'll have built the foundation for an enormous constellation of personal skills and accomplishments that I call your "skills arsenal." In this chapter, we'll take an inventory of your skills. What are your general skills? Your job-specific skills? Your personal traits that add value? Your areas of exceptional competency? Your special gifts and talents that make you unique?

Building those "stories" from your list of skills is something we'll tackle together in Chapter 3, where you will learn the most concise and powerful way to verbally express your skills—the Q statement. No question will be able to catch you off guard because you will always be prepared to offer stories about accomplishments that will impress and maybe even dazzle the interviewer.

In this chapter we'll be discussing five types of skills:

- General skills
- Job-specific skills
- Personal traits
- Competencies
- Gifts

Identifying your skills in each of these categories is the first step in crafting stories and examples that will help you explain your skills and experience to interviewers clearly in a convincing (and interesting) way.

General Skills

First, let's take a look at general skills and see why they can be so important to you in the interview, whether you're planning to stay in the same occupation or you're thinking about making a move into an entirely new profession or a new industry.

Using General Skills in an Interview for a Career Change

"Managing" is one example of a general skill. It is called a "general skill" because it can be found in almost every industry—sports, computers, retail, manufacturing, health care, and even entertainment. And occupations like sales manager, department manager, production manager, project manager, program manager, office manager, and accounts manager require the use of management skills.

One exciting outcome of taking stock of your general skills is that it will enable you to link the set of skills you have developed in one career to the set of skills required in a different career. Someone who has managed budgets, inventory, and teams of people in the computer hardware field might find that he or she can apply those skills in another industry such as manufacturing.

In other words, if you wanted to make a jump from being a project manager in engineering to being a production manager in the film industry, *you would not be at a loss for some of the most important general skills required for that kind of change.* In the process, however, you would probably be required to answer an interviewer's questions about your abilities to make that kind of change. Your answer might look something like this:

> Although I have not had direct experience in the film industry yet, I do have management skills. I have managed budgets of up to $1 million, teams of up to 48 engineers and technicians, and schedules involving up to three different projects, each on different deadlines. Through creative scheduling and careful allocation of resources, I was able to bring one project in 18 days ahead of the deadline, thereby saving my company over $147,000. That's exactly the kind of savings I'd like to bring to your film company.

Holly, one of my clients, was a teacher, but she was able to make a career change into the much more highly paid field of training and development for a human resources department of a large computer firm. Though the occupations were different, she was able to identify several important general skills that they shared. Her general skills list looked like this:

- Curriculum planning
- Research
- Presentations
- Teaching
- Evaluation

When the human resources director asked her how she thought she could apply her teaching skills to training, Holly said something like this:

> When I took over the fourth-grade class at Bowden Street Elementary in Minneapolis, the grade point average for the preceding 5 years had been a C minus. Using my skills in researching age-appropriate program planning, interactive learning approaches, and developing innovative presentations, I was able to bring up the class average to a B plus. It's an achievement I'm very proud of—just the kind of improvement I expect to make in your employee morale and performance.

Using General Skills to Get a New Job

General skills can, of course, also be used when you are applying for the same type of job in the same type of industry. If you were applying for a job of a social work case manager at an agency where the caseload was particularly heavy, you might want to emphasize some of your general skills having to do with organization. Suppose your list of general skills looked like this:

- Assessing
- Counseling
- Researching
- Reporting
- Coordinating
- Organizing

If an interviewer were to ask you, "What are your strengths?" you might choose to answer in the following way, *introducing* your three most salient strengths and then *elaborating* on one of the strengths, such as in the answer cited below:

QUESTION: *What are your greatest strengths?*

ANSWER: Well, some of my greatest strengths lie in the areas of counseling, reporting, and organization. An example of an experience in which my organizational skills were very important is a position I had with Ford Human Services in Richmond, Virginia. I was responsible for a caseload of over 75 clients, which meant that I had to keep careful notes and records, and, of course, I had to review these notes before each meeting with a client. I was commended for the attention to detail in my reports, which I was able to provide because I had kept such well-organized files on my clients. I am proud that because of my organizational skills, I was able to handle such a large client base. I'm confident I will give your clients the same level of respect and detailed, indepth attention.

You can see a pattern emerging:

1. You mention *three* skills that you used in a prior job that would also be of value in your next occupation. (We'll discover, in Chapter 8, how to assess which skills are important to your interviewer.)

2. You pick *one* skill that you believe would be *most important* for the particular job you're applying for.

3. You tell a very short story about that particular skill. You can elaborate on this story by providing specific numbers, percentages, feedback, rankings, and dollar amounts. (We're going to explore this technique more fully in Chapter 3 on Q statements.)

4. You mention that you are proud of your achievement.

5. You link your past accomplishments or results with your future performance at the company you're applying for, by saying, "And that's exactly what I'd like to do for your company." (We'll talk about why this is so important in Chapter 5.)

General Skills Inventory

Now it's time for you to take a look at the general skills you possess:

1. Scan the following list of general skills.
2. Make a checkmark next to those skills you have used reasonably well. It's possible that you have used a skill only once but are still reasonably proficient with it so that you could use it again if you had the chance.

    Be generous with yourself as you decide whether you have these skills. You need not be an expert in them, nor is it necessary that you have used them in a work environment. Think carefully back to school, recreational, social, or volunteer situations in which you may have used these skills:

___ Advertising

___ Advising

___ Analyzing data

___ Analyzing situations

___ Arranging events

___ Assessing performance

___ Assessing progress

___ Assessing quality

___ Assisting

___ Attending to detail

___ Auditing

___ Building structures

___ Building relationships

___ Building credibility

___ Building cooperation

___ Budgeting

___ Calculating

___ Classifying

___ Client relations

___ Coaching

___ Corresponding

___ Communicating in writing

___ Communicating verbally

___ Communicating nonverbally

___ Communicating feelings

___ Communicating ideas

___ Communicating instructions

___ Conceptualizing

___ Consulting

___ Correcting

___ Counseling

___ Data processing

___ Decision making

___ Decorating

___ Delegating

___ Developing systems

___ Developing designs

___ Developing talent

___ Diagnosing

___ Directing

___ Drafting

___ Drawing

___ Driving

___ Editing

___ Educating

___ Empathizing

___ Enforcing

___ Engineering

___ Evaluating

___ Filing

___ Financial planning

___ Forecasting

___ Formulating

___ Fund raising

___ Healing

___ Helping others

___ Implementing

___ Imagining

___ Influencing

___ Initiating

___ Intuiting

___ Intervening

___ Inventing

___ Investigating

___ Leading people

___ Lecturing

___ Lifting

___ Listening

___ Managing tasks

___ Marketing

___ Marketing and communications

___ Massaging

___ Nurturing

___ Observing

___ Operating computers

___ Organizing

___ Prescribing

___ Program managing

___ Programming computers

___ Project managing

___ Promoting

___ Public speaking

___ Recording

___ Repairing

___ Reconstructing

___ Reporting

___ Researching

___ Sales and marketing

___ Selling

___ Servicing equipment

___ Servicing customers

___ Supervising

___ Surveying

___ Team building

___ Team leading

___ Telephone calling

___ Tending

___ Tooling

___ Training

___ Troubleshooting

___ Understanding

___ Using equipment

___ Using the Internet

Other general skills not mentioned

_____

_____

_____

_____

_____

_____

_____

_____

_____

3. Now, go back over the list again from beginning to end. This time around, *circle* those skills that are checked off *and* that you want to *continue* to use in your next job.

4. Now you have a list in which some of the skills have *both* a checkmark *and* a circle, which means the following:

   a. You can use them.

   b. You like to use them.

   c. You would like to *continue* to use them in your next job.

5. There is one more step, and this is the most challenging one yet. Pick out *six* of the skills that you have on the your list that are circled *and* checkmarked.

When it comes to narrowing the number of your skills down to six, it's likely that you may be thinking, "I'd like to use almost all of these skills. I enjoy using them so much that I hate to narrow the list down to just six." Think about this for a moment: The last time you bought or leased a car, did you actually consider *every single* feature the car had—from the axle to the hoses to the spark plugs to the tail lights?

Would you have been enticed to purchase the car if the advertisement or the salesperson had just said "This car has all features" and did nothing to explain specifically what the most important features of the car were?

Wouldn't it have been more engaging if the advertisement or salesperson had mentioned six or seven *special* features that you were actually looking for, like air-conditioning, an audio system with six speakers, or a 5-year unconditional factory warranty?

> ***The "special features" on this car are like the selected skills you bring with you to the interview.***

By mentioning the "features" you *know* you have and you know the employer wants, you show the employer that you're equipped to solve the kinds of problems inherent in the job. (We'll learn some easy ways to determine *which* skills are important to the employer in Chapter 4 on the topic of research.)

Job-Specific Skills

You may be saying, "Fine, I'm a manager with good organizational skills, but there's a lot more to my job than that!" You're right. You have very specific knowledge and expertise that you use in your particular vocation. Job-specific skills are those abilities that you need to succeed in your particular job in your particular company in your particular industry. These are the abilities that another person who has the same job title as yours would have to have to meet the job's basic requirements.

Scan the lines below for some examples of job-specific skills for different occupations. You may not see *your* occupation listed, but you'll get an idea of the difference between these skills and the general skills we talked about before. Your job specific skills are usually listed on your résumé, but remember the key to interviewing: It's not enough just to *possess* a skill or even have it written on your résumé. You have to be able to *verbally express* it.

Please take a look at the following list of some job-specific skills areas in which proficiency is necessary in these selected occupations. I think you'll see how they differ from general skills:

Occupation	Selected Job-Specific Skills
Accountant	Accounts payable Accounts receivable Payroll
Marketing specialist	Press release writing Trade-show coordinating Forecasting
Financial advisor	Series 7 license Knowledge of stocks, bonds, mutual funds Knowledge of retirement planning and living trusts
Football player	Understanding football strategy Staying in shape off season Playing the position (quarterback, linebacker, tight end)
Environmental planner	Knowledge of geology and biology Knowledge of causes and treatments for pollutants Knowledge of the ecology of a given geographic area
Semiconductor assembler	Component parts of a wafer Clean-room and safety procedures Superior fine-motor control
Psychotherapist	Diagnosis of a client's health Knowledge of nonverbal behavior Cognitive-behavioral therapy techniques
Publisher	Exceptional literacy The publishing process from "pitching" to marketing How to evaluate books for publication
Computer programmer	Computer languages Computer platforms C, SQL, Perl, Java, JavaScript

Occupation	Selected Job-Specific Skills
Surgeon	Knowledge of human anatomy and physiology How to make a diagnosis and prognosis Ability to perform surgery
Office manager	Order office supplies within a budget Microsoft Office, Lotus, Peachtree software Operation of multi-line phone system

Now I'd like you to try your hand at identifying some of the job-specific skills *you* possess.

Job-Specific Skills Inventory

List 6 to 10 of your job-specific skills here. What abilities must you possess to get a job in your chosen industry? It's helpful if the skills you include are those in the job description for the new position you're interviewing for. When the employer asks you the inevitable questions, "What are your strengths?" and "What are your skills?" you will have the best of your skills for that job right at your fingertips.

1. _____

_____

2. _____

_____

3. _____

_____

4. _____

_____

5. _____

_____

6. _____

_____

7. _____

_____

8. _____

_____

9. _____

_____

10. _____

_____

Personal Traits

Great! Now we're ready to move on to another set of skills called personal traits. They are every bit as important as your general skills, and they usually make up a set of personal characteristics that you possess. These skills have more to do with who you *are* than what you *do*, and they bear heavily upon your attitude, your work habits, your ethics, and the way you relate to other people.

When the employer asks a question like "What would your former boss have to say about you?" or "What did your former coworkers think of you?" it's very useful to be able to describe yourself using three or four of the adjectives in the next exercise.

Personal Traits Inventory

Go through the following list twice. The first time, go through the list and place a checkmark beside the traits that apply to you. *There's nothing to be gained from being modest.* If you asked any good friend or coworker, he or she would probably agree that you do, indeed, possess those qualities!

___ Accepting	___ Diligent
___ Accurate	___ Diplomatic
___ Achievement oriented	___ Direct
___ Action oriented	___ Driven
___ Aggressive	___ Dynamic
___ Ambitious	___ Economical
___ Analytical	___ Effective
___ Artistic	___ Efficient
___ Assertive	___ Emotionally strong
___ Aware	___ Energetic
___ Balanced	___ Entertaining
___ Brilliant	___ Enthusiastic
___ Businesslike	___ Entrepreneurial
___ Calm	___ Ethical
___ Caring	___ Exemplary
___ Challenging	___ Expressive
___ Charismatic	___ Fair
___ Committed	___ Friendly
___ Communicative	___ Generous
___ Compassionate	___ Genuine
___ Competitive	___ Gifted
___ Concerned	___ Hard working
___ Confident	___ Helpful
___ Considerate	___ Honest
___ Courageous	___ Humorous
___ Courteous	___ Independent
___ Creative	___ Innovative
___ Dedicated	___ Insightful
___ Dependable	___ Inspirational
___ Detail oriented	___ Intellectual
___ Determined	___ Intelligent

___ Intuitive
___ Inventive
___ Knowledgeable
___ Logical
___ Loyal
___ Mature
___ Methodical
___ Meticulous
___ Modest
___ Motivating
___ Nurturing
___ Observant
___ Optimistic
___ Orderly
___ Organized
___ Outgoing
___ Patient
___ Perfectionistic
___ Persuasive
___ Physically strong
___ Private
___ Proactive
___ Productive
___ Punctual
___ Rational
___ Relaxed
___ Reserved
___ Resilient
___ Resourceful
___ Respected
___ Respectful

___ Responsible
___ Responsive
___ Results oriented
___ Scientific
___ Self-controlled
___ Self-motivated
___ Sincere
___ Sociable
___ Spontaneous
___ Supportive
___ Systematic
___ Tactful
___ Task oriented
___ Team oriented
___ Tenacious
___ Thorough
___ Tidy
___ Tolerant
___ Trustworthy
___ Uninhibited
___ Unselfish
___ Unstoppable
___ Unusual
___ Verbal
___ Versatile
___ Visionary
___ Warm
___ Well groomed
___ Well liked
___ Well spoken

The second time you go through the list, please select the three or four personal traits that describe you best and that you think you would like to use in your next job. You may very well possess a majority of these skills. To narrow them down for the following list, try to list those traits that seem to come to you almost naturally and effortlessly. You might also consider listing the traits you're most often complimented for. Please record them here:

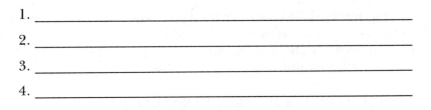

Competencies

You've already uncovered some foundational skills that will surely impress your interviewer and tip the scales in your direction— your general skills, your job-specific skills, and your personal traits. Now, let's add two more types of skills that will add even more credibility to your presentation.

The first is a group of skills called *competencies*. Competencies are actually clusters of skills, and they are rapidly becoming the criteria upon which *all* employees and potential employees are judged. They can make the difference between being promoted or passed over. They can and definitely do carve out the space between people who are hired and those who are not. More and more, *interviewers are trained to look at competencies as well as skills*.

The Occupational Outlook Handbook, a useful source for career information, is updated and published yearly by the U.S. Department of Labor. It lists the job descriptions, qualifications, job market expectancies, and salaries for more than 6000 jobs, and it is published both nationally and regionally. Accessing it on the Internet at www.bls.gov/oco/ or in hard copy at your local library is a top-notch way to find vast information on what kinds of skills, education, personal traits, and competencies employers are looking for to fulfill certain positions. Increasingly, the *hand-*

book is listing competencies as well as skills to draw a well-rounded picture of what employers actually demand.

For example, the *handbook* notes that for the position of "financial and securities advisor," such competencies and personal traits as "a desire to succeed," "ability to handle rejection," and "self-confidence" may actually be of *more* value to the employer than traditional skills like numerical ability or formal education.

Even in positions involving a very high level of technical skill, competencies still come strongly into play. In a Web site job description of skills necessary for a computer hardware engineer, "willingness to constantly update knowledge" is a competency that ranks as high in importance as other skills that are more technology oriented.

What Are Some of the Most Valued Competencies?

Some of the core competencies that are most important for many positions in today's rapidly shifting marketplace are the following:

- *Flexibility.* The ability to change, sometimes quickly, from one set of job duties to another, or from one team to another or to working extra or different hours.

- *Adaptability.* The ability to tolerate and maximize the potential of large organizational shifts such as mergers or layoffs. Also, the ability to adjust to new leadership and management—to change departments, divisions, locations, or job titles.

- *Problem-solving skills.* The ability to self-correct. Having the tendency to tackle problems independently and with a minimum of supervision. Having the ability to tolerate frustration and/or failure until the solution to the problem is found. Maintaining persistence despite ambiguous or incomplete information and perseverance despite initial failure or frustration.

- *Interpersonal communication.* The ability to communicate in a way that is appropriate to company culture as well as individual preferences, with empathy, clarity, and good listening behaviors. Having the ability to give feedback and having sensitivity to multicultural preferences in communication style. Being technologically literate and able to utilize the latest forms of written and electronic communication.

- *Ability and willingness to learn.* A willingness to attend professional development workshops and seminars. The ability to self-correct and alter one's own behavior. Having a propensity to pursue outside sources of formal and informal education, and taking personal responsibility to remain abreast of advances in one's field or occupation.

I once had the CEO of a high-tech company tell me that, he personally considered adaptability to be the most important quality any of his employees could possess and that he would not hire (and would even fire) those who could not demonstrate it!

Employers are very unlikely to ask you directly whether or not you possess these skills, yet they will be looking for them in your demeanor, in the stories you tell, and in the way you tell them.

You'll be taking an inventory of your competencies in the next chapter, where I'll ask you to provide an example or "story" about how you've used each of them. In Chapter 4, you'll learn how you can adjust your competencies to match those most valued by the company by aligning them with the company mission and company culture.

Your Gift

The last skill I would like to talk about is simply what I call a "gift." It's not something you learned or something you read about. It's much more about *who you are* than *what you do*. It may have been with you since birth. Perhaps it's genetically inscribed, divinely bestowed, or perhaps part of the fabric of very early childhood experiences.

What's important about knowing your gift is that, consciously or not, it's the most compelling thing about you. It's like the sun around which all the other stars and planets of your skills revolve. Your interviewer may not be able to give it a name, but he or she will feel it when you are relaxed, easy, and natural, which is what this book is preparing you to be. Do you have a hunch what *your* gift may be?

- *What is the thing that people most often compliment you for?* Is it your wit or intelligence? Is it the ability to find humor in any situation?
- *What is a quality that you would never, under any circumstances, give up?* Is it your passion or intensity? Is it your rationality? Your devotion?
- *What quality would you like to be remembered for after your death?* Is it your perseverance against all odds? Is it your ability to inspire others? Your brilliance? Your compassion? Your technical expertise? Your leadership?
- *Is your gift . . .* Your kindness? Your refined artistic taste? Your vision? Your generosity?

Take a while and think about *your* gift. Along with all these externally oriented skills you have identified in this chapter, see if you can also bring some of this gift in to the interview. Your gift makes up some of what we call your *chemistry* with another person. If it's worth having (which it is), it's worth sharing.

Skills Summary Page

List the 6 skills you picked from your general skills list:

1. _____
2. _____
3. _____
4. _____
5. _____
6. _____

List your 6 to 10 job-specific skills:

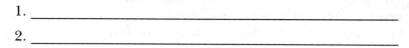

1. _____
2. _____

3. _____

4. _____

5. _____

6. _____

7. _____

8. _____

9. _____

10. _____

List your 3 to 4 strongest personal traits:

1. _____

2. _____

3. _____

4. _____

List your three top competencies:

1. _____

2. _____

3. _____

Write a few sentences about your gift.

_____

_____

_____

_____

_____

_____

I'd like you to carefully read through what you've just written. I am willing to bet, right now, that there is not another person on this planet who has the exact same list as you have, with the exact same stories to tell about how and where they used their skills.

In fact, your skills arsenal is as unique as you are. *Your talents are to be treasured.* I hope you give yourself a good, hearty pat on the back! The following chapters will help you make sure you can convince an employer that you deserve to be paid well for your particular package of talents.

CHAPTER THREE

Q Statements: Your Secret Weapon

Each of us has some unique capability, waiting for realization.

—George H. Bender

In the last chapter, you identified your skills, personal traits, competencies, and gifts—a task that's surprisingly difficult for most job seekers. In fact, this crucial bit of "homework" puts you well ahead of most other job applicants. It's an essential step toward your ultimate goal—being able to clearly describe your skills and qualifications to an interviewer. The next step will be to use these skills to create pithy, memorable, quantifiable "sound bytes" about yourself, assertions we'll call *Q statements*.

What Is a Q Statement?

A *Q statement* is a sentence (or group of sentences) that expresses a *numerical measurement* of some action or accomplishment you have performed. It is quantitative. A Q statement is not vague; it's exact. For example, rather than saying you "increased productivity," using a Q statement, you would say that you "increased productivity by 25 percent."

Why quantify a skill? Let's take a look at the following statements and see which of them bears the most weight and leaves the longest-lasting impression:

STATEMENT A: I am a good communicator.

STATEMENT B: I have lectured to more than 12,000 people worldwide on the topic of personal financial planning, and I have worked individually with clients from 19 to 90 years old.

Which of these two statements seems the most evocative? From which one can you make a mental picture? Which will you remember?

Statement B is more descriptive and more concrete. It does not simply make a claim or advance a personal opinion. Statement B uses actual facts and numbers to specifically *demonstrate* the skills. This kind of clarification gives the listener evidence of the skill and a good idea of the scope of it.

Let's take another example:

STATEMENT A: I'm an excellent manager.

STATEMENT B: I have managed 135 people on projects budgeted for over $2.1 million.

41

> ### *Remember, this is not bragging.*
> ### *These are facts.*

If you really *do* have an accomplishment of such magnitude as the one above, which statement would serve you better? Which statement would help the interviewer to make the best decision about your qualifications? While "I'm an excellent manager" is a fine thing to say, it would be a lot stronger if it were supported by statement B.

Interviewers these days *want* to hear specific data. If you don't provide the interviewer with concrete, quantified examples of what you did, the interviewer will very likely ask you to. It's much more impressive to be prepared to offer them yourself, without prompting. And in the opposite direction, it is most troubling if the employer asks for examples of your skills and you can't think of any. To prevent being caught off guard this way, you'll want to prepare several Q statements (targeted to each specific job) before every interview. If you can learn how to quantify your skills *now*, it will become an ingrained habit, at your command whenever you need to use it.

Let's take a look at the structure and content of some other concrete, quantified statements:

- Since I've become the director of operations, I've been responsible for helping the company to decrease waste by 20 percent, resulting in an overall savings of $1.2 million a year.
- I ran a bicycle sales and repair store with 17employees and gross annual sales of $193,000.
- I operated a multiline phone system and personally handled over 200 calls per day.
- Since I took over as the CEO of this pharmaceuticals company, we have gone from number 347 to number 197 in the list of Fortune 500 companies.
- As a program manager, I instituted and developed a production process that increased profits by 42 percent in the second quarter.

- I acted as a regional manager for 12 offices overseeing 147 salespeople throughout the Midwest.
- As a human resources manager, I initiated and developed a retraining program that improved employee satisfaction from 2.7 to 4.1 on a scale of 1 to 5.
- As a production manager, I decreased production time by 6 days a month, resulting in a savings of $360,000 quarterly.
- I maintain a caseload of 65 patients.
- I built a prototype that could tolerate 15 percent more stress than its predecessor.
- My team identified four as-yet-unknown species of flora and fauna in the mountainous regions of California.
- I reduced overhead by 25 percent while increasing profits by 43 percent annually.
- I designed a microchip that is 23 percent more reliable than its predecessor.
- I introduced an on-site safety program that decreased workers' compensation claims by 18 percent in 1 year.
- I process more than 250 customer requests daily.
- I won an award for decreasing materials costs from $6.41 per inch to $5.20 per inch.
- I have overseen the landscape design on over 200 projects, costing up to $350,000 per project.

After reading all these different Q statements, you probably see a pattern emerging. First, they all contain action words—verbs such as *designed*, *initiated*, *saved*, *processed*, and *handled*. Second, they all end with some sort of number, expressed in monetary amounts, time, and percentages, and numerical amounts of people, actions, or things.

The "formula" for a Q statement would look something like this:

Verb + (who, what, when, where, how) + Result = Q statement

Notice that the results are *specific, concrete,* and *measurable.* And notice that, they all, at the bottom line, lead to some sort of direct benefit or monetary profit to the company.

There are five ways to quantify your accomplishments:

1. By numbers of people, places, things, units, or actions, such as "handled 200 telephone calls per day."
2. By amounts of money saved or earned, such as "$300,000 savings" or "$100,000 in profits."
3. In percentages (or fractions), such as "70 percent decrease in waste", or "33 percent increase in production."
4. By time saved, which usually means money saved.
5. By a subjective or objective scale or rank, such as "4.8 on a scale of 1 to 5 for increased customer satisfaction" or "moving from number 360 to number 121 on the Fortune 500 list."

Quality or Quantity?

Of course, it would be absurd to try to quantify every single one of your tasks or accomplishments. Still, at the very least, you can be *qualitatively* specific. For example, instead of simply saying, "I'm multilingual," you could say, "I am fluent in French, Spanish, and Chinese." Or, instead of saying that your artwork has been shown in "many galleries," you might say that your work has been shown in "galleries in Los Angeles, San Francisco, Santa Fe, Denver, and New York."

Other statements that do not need to be quantified to convey the weight of accomplishment would be the following:

- I won an award for being the employee of the year.
- I'm president of the Society for Historical Research.
- I graduated with highest honors.
- My customers have described me as dependable, honest, and fair.
- My last boss would describe me as dynamic, innovative, and creative.

- I created a new curriculum for self-esteem in secondary schools.
- I invented a new type of kitchen sponge.

Let's Get Specific

We'll talk more about qualitative statements later in this chapter, but for now we'll stick with learning more about Q statements. Now that you've read quite a few Q statements, let's move on to creating some of your own. It's time to look back at the list of your general skills in Chapter 2. Let's say "organize" is at the top of your list. An *unspecific statement* might look like this:

I am very organized.

A *more specific statement* would look like this:

I organized meetings for top international executives in New York, Washington, D.C., and Hong Kong.

The *quantified* version of this statement would look like this:

I organized up to 40 meetings a week for over 15 international executives in New York, Washington, D.C., and Hong Kong.

Q Statements for General Skills

Now that you have a Q statement, use the skills that you unearthed in Chapter 2 to construct two or three Q statements of your own for each general skill that you chose. Add additional ones as you think of more of your quantified accomplishments.

Please note your ideas on the next few pages.

Skill 1 _____ (name of skill)

Q statement:

_____

_____

_____

Q statement:

_____

_____

_____

Q statement:

_____

_____

_____

Skill 2 _____ (name of skill)

Q statement:

_____

_____

_____

Q statement:

_____

_____

_____

Q statement:

_____

_____

_____

Skill 3 _____ (name of skill)

Q statement:

_____

_____

_____

Q statement:

_____

_____

_____

Q statement:

_____

_____

_____

Skill 4 _____ (name of skill)

Q statement:

_____

_____

_____

Q statement:

_____

_____

_____

Q statement:

_____

_____

_____

Skill 5 _____ (name of skill)

Q statement:

_____

_____

_____

Q statement:

_____

_____

_____

Q statement:

_____

_____

_____

Skill 6 _____ (name of skill)

Q statement:

_____

_____

_____

Q statement:

_____

_____

_____

Q statement:

_____

_____

_____

Great! You now have some powerful statements to use as real-life examples of how you can contribute to the bottom-line profits of a company. You can prove to the interviewer that you can produce results—because *if you have done it once, it's a good bet that you can do it again.*

Q Statements for Job-Specific Skills

Now that you've made your general skills "leap off the page," I'd like you to do the same for your job-specific skills. If you can't quantify them, try just thinking of an example, story, or situation in which you used the skill.

The more vivid the story, the more credible it will seem to the interviewer!

Please use the worksheet that follows to keep a record of your examples:

Skill 1 _____ (name of skill)

Q statement:

_____

_____

_____

Q statement:

_____

_____

_____

Q statement:

_____

_____

_____

Skill 2 _____ (name of skill)

Q statement:

_____

_____

_____

Q statement:

_____

_____

_____

Q statement:

_____

_____

_____

Skill 3 _____ (name of skill)

Q statement:

_____

_____

_____

Q statement:

_____

_____

_____

Q statement:

_____

_____

_____

Skill 4 _____ (name of skill)

Q statement:

_____

_____

_____

Q statement:

_____

_____

_____

Q statement:

_____

_____

_____

Skill 5 _____ (name of skill)

Q statement:

_____

_____

_____

Q statement:

_____

_____

_____

Q statement:

_____

_____

_____

Skill 6 _____ (name of skill)

Q statement:

_____

_____

_____

Q statement:

_____

_____

_____

Q statement:

_____

_____

_____

Q Statements for Personal Traits

After taking a breather from all of those incredible accomplishments, let's take a look at some of the more intangible qualities you bring to the interview—your personal traits. There are specific ways to *make these skills come alive* in the eyes of the employer too.

Let's say that one of your personal traits is that you're dependable. That's an important attribute, but it's difficult to quantify. However, you may have an anecdote or short story that *demonstrates* that you are dependable. To express the quality of dependability, you might say something like this:

> I'm very dependable. Every time the boss left the plant to go out on business, he left the operations of the plant and responsibility for the crew up to me.

You might also say:

> I'm very dependable. In 2 years of working for this company, I haven't once been late for an appointment with a customer.

> **As is true when talking about your general skills, it's not wise to make a claim about your personal traits without having some evidence to support it. Try to find at least one story, fact, example, or anecdote that proves you have that trait.**

Please return to your skills summary page in Chapter 2, and find the list of your three to four personal traits. Write at least one example of when you demonstrated that trait or used that skill. Use the following pages to keep a record.

Personal trait 1 _____ (name of trait)

Q statement:

_____

_____

_____

Personal trait 2 _____ (name of trait)

Q statement:

_____

_____

_____

Personal trait 3 _____ (name of trait)

Q statement:

_____

_____

_____

Q Statements for Competencies

The same technique can be used to demonstrate your competencies. Again, return to the skills summary page in Chapter 2. Find examples of how you demonstrated three of those essential competencies and describe them here. *They need not have been used in a work setting.* All that's important is that you have an example or anecdote about how you used them in the past.

Competency 1 _____ (name of competency)

Q statement:

_____

_____

_____

Competency 2 _____ (name of competency)

Q statement:

_____

_____

_____

Competency 3 _____ (name of competency)

Q statement:

_____

_____

_____

Q Statements for Your Gift

Refer again to your skills summary page and see if you can be even more specific about how you've used your gift. Again, it's not necessary that you used this skill in a work setting, only that you can demonstrate it through some concrete example.

Your gift: _____

Q statement:

_____

_____

_____

Excellent work! Believe it or not, you are almost ready for your interview. The next chapter will give you a few more helpful hints on preparation before you stride into the interviewer's office.

CHAPTER FOUR

Research: What Separates the Hired from the Not Hired

> *Great works are performed not by strength, but by perseverance.*
>
> —Samuel Johnson

An Interview Is Like a First Date

Have you ever been on a first date with a guy who talked *only* about himself? With a woman who never asked you any questions about *your* life or *your* interests? This person just blabbed on about himself or herself until the end of the evening, when you were relieved that it was finally O-V-E-R. Unless you were interested in getting to know an egomaniac, it's likely that the first date was probably the last.

An interview is a lot like a first date, in that displaying interest in the other person (in this case, the company) actually makes you *more attractive* to the person. It's flattering if you ask the person questions that allow them to "brag" a little bit. It's a pleasant surprise to the other person if you show that you actually know a little bit about some of the things that are important to him or her.

Why Research a Company?

This chapter will present a deep well of resources from which to plumb information on just about any company, large or small. Besides enabling you to "flatter" the interviewer, there are at least six central reasons to research a company before you step into the interview:

1. To find out whether or not it's a place you want to work
2. To discover what skills the job or the company most values
3. To ferret out as much as you can about the company culture and mission in order to align some of your competencies to fit the company's style and goals
4. To impress the employer when he or she asks: "Tell me, what do you know about our company, and why would you like to work here?"
5. So you can make intelligent queries when the employer asks you: "So, do you have any questions about our company?"
6. To give you an advantage because your competitors for this job are *not* researching the company to the degree that you're going to

All the Information Is Right at Your Fingertips

Think you'll never find out anything about Company XYZ because it's too small, it's highly secretive, or it doesn't have a Web site? Think again. There are people who have full-time jobs gathering information (including information about extremely private topics, like salaries of certain employees) on just about any company you can imagine.

You can locate facts and opinions about companies in a number of ways:

- From company Web sites
- Through other research on the Internet
- From proprietary, or "for-fee," databases
- From public, or "free," databases
- From one-stop job centers around the country
- In public libraries, from their books, periodicals, and computer databases
- From the interviewer, *during the interview itself!*

Can you think of any others? When you put your mind to it, there seem to be countless ways to gather information if you have just a couple of hours and the inclination to hunt for it.

How to Get Your Hands on a Computer

If you own a computer, you're in luck, but if you don't, you can easily locate one you can use for free or for a small fee at one of the following spots:

- At a computer café that charges low fees by the minute or hour
- At a public library—for free!
- At a copy center, like Kinko's
- At a local one-stop career center, if you qualify for services

A note about career centers: One-stop career centers were created for public use by the U.S. federal government in the 1990s. They can be found in every large city and many medium-sized towns across the nation. You can also participate in their free workshops on résumés, interviewing, and other job-related topics as well as obtain limited one-to-one support with a career counselor.

Because they are founded and maintained by government funding, you have to call first to see if you qualify for services. Don't count yourself out! I've seen everyone from secretaries to CEOs to writers and actors utilizing one-stop career centers. If you need to use a computer for research or wish to further investigate their offerings, go to the Internet address provided below.

If you were laid off from your last position, you definitely qualify to use these career centers. You may also be qualified for other reasons, such as income, family situation, veteran's status, age, disability, substance abuse history, and many more.

Keep in mind that one-stops are not only a place to use a free computer—they are also a terrific resource and source of support for just about every job seeker.

> **You can get in touch with one of the many thousands of one-stop career centers around the United States to see if you are qualified to use their services.**

---

1. On a computer, go to the following:
   http://www.usworkforce.org/onestop.
2. On the first page, click on the link "one-stop Web sites."
3. You'll be taken to a page that displays a map of the United States.
   Click on your state.
4. This will bring up a new Web site dedicated to your state.
5. Continue to click on: "one-stop sites," "one-stop locations," "local one-stop centers," "one-stop maps," or "one-stop directions" until you find the names, phone numbers, and other contact information for centers near you.

I bet you're in front of a computer just about now and ready to launch the hunt! Let's pick a relatively easy company to research first, such as a large Fortune 500 company.

Company Web Sites

Almost every large company has a Web site (usually www.their-companyname.com). Many medium and very small (even one-person) companies also have a presence on the Web. The key is finding them.

Some companies will have Web sites with initials that stand for the name such as www.abc.com standing for "American Business Center." Instead of guessing, though, I suggest that you save time and go to a major search engine like Google (www.google.com) and enter the company name (in full) as your search term. This will bring you directly to a link you can click on to go to the company Web site.

Explore the site. Notice both the content *and* the "feel" of the site. Is it leaning toward a traditional type of design or toward a bold modern design? This alone may tell you a little bit about the personality of the company. What is the company message or mission? Does it have a slogan or catch phrase that reveals its philosophy? What products or services does it offer? How large is the company, and when was it founded? Who is the CEO or some of the other executive members?

Are there any names of women in those ranks? Is it very, or not at all, important to you that women be leaders of a company this size? Where does the company appear to be moving? Is it announcing any new product or service lines? What is the general feeling or attitude it seems to project regarding its customers? How about its employees?

Company Mission Statements

Steven Beasley, one of the leading researchers and lecturers on competencies in the world, counsels job candidates to *"align their competencies with the mission of the company"* for the best interviewing results.

Here's an actual mission statement from a leading Internet company that clearly spells out some of the competencies it expects from its employees. This mission statement was plainly written on their Web site.

> It is our goal to foster an environment of *creativity* and *cooperation*, where each employee can participate in the company mission: to create, and *continue to improve* upon, a product that serves the community and the world as a leader in the pursuit of knowledge and information.

Remember our list of personal traits in Chapter 2? This company is telling you right here in its mission statement what it is looking for.

Having read and absorbed the mission statement, you might want to emphasize the following qualities (and others you have that seem to match their values) if you were seeking employment there:

- Creative
- Self-motivated
- Innovative
- Team oriented
- Experienced in handling interpersonal communication
- Inventive
- Experienced in problem solving

Company Culture

By *company culture* we mean the *norms of behavior* (formal, informal, competitive, cooperative) that are or are not expected or offered in the everyday work environment. Company culture may refer to many things such as the following:

- Manner of dress (formal business attire versus casual dress)
- Means of communication (e-mail, phone, or just dropping by someone's office)
- Treatment of superiors, subordinates, and peers
- Use of first names or last names

- Work ethic and work hours
- Frequency and ease of promotions
- "Unwritten" behavior required for social acceptance
- Tolerance of differences
- Demands for conformity
- Fun or recreational time allowed during working hours
- Multicultural, sexual preference, and gender sensitivity
- Openness or secretiveness of management

It may include perks like free food or beverages on site, free dry-cleaning pickup, recreation rooms, health club memberships, or fitness classes.

Company culture information can often be gleaned from a company's Web site. One tech company, for example, uses its Web site to describe the company culture in the following way:

- All the snacks you can eat
- Free gourmet lunches served daily
- Free massage therapy
- Roller hockey
- Game room
- Gym

Now I bet half of you reading this book would like to pack up and work for this company right now! (It must be the roller hockey!) But what about those of you who don't necessarily believe in mixing work with play and who wouldn't mind bringing a bag lunch to an environment that's a bit less stressful? (Free food usually means long hours.) And maybe you'd prefer to work for a company in which the pace was a bit slower instead of high-energy, and highly demanding.

I wouldn't suggest that you decline an interview there just because of what the Web site says, but it might be *one* component of your final decision about whether or not to accept a job offer from that company (something we'll discuss in depth in Chapter 10).

Targeting Your Skills to the Company's Needs

Go to the Web site of a company that you're interested in working for. If you don't know of any companies that fit the bill, go to www.hoovers.com. In the site search section, chose "search by industry." Then enter the name of an industry you're targeting, like "fashion." Hoovers will come up with a long, healthy list of companies for you to investigate, including the corporate Web address for each of those companies.

When you've gotten to the corporate Web page of a company you'd like to explore, have a look at the section of the Web site that is announcing current job openings. Is your job there? What kinds of specific words are used to describe the job title and its responsibilities as well as the requirements for skills and education, and especially personal traits and competencies?

Now look back at your skills summary page in Chapter 2. Are your skills a good fit with this company, or do you think that you might need to pick out some other skills from your arsenal to emphasize to this particular employer?

After exploring the whole Web site, what are the personal traits and competencies that appear to be called for by this company and this job?

Is the company looking for loyalty or risk taking? Does it prefer the use of time-tested conventional methods or innovation? Is the company looking for highly independent or more team oriented people? Do they expect you to come in and "hit the ground running" or learn more slowly as you go?

Researching a company from information that *they* supply in print or on the Web can obviously put you way ahead of the competition—and more at ease in the interview, because you know whom you're talking to.

There is, however, something missing when you operate only from the information that the company *wants* you to hear about it. It's important to also look at what other people are saying about this company—analysts and others in the media who know the industry and this company's place in it.

What do major magazines and newspapers and financial and business analysts have to say about these organizations—their stability, their treatment of employees, their place among their competitors, or their outlook for the future? Here are a few things you might look for in others' assessment of a company:

- Is this a company that is in a major union dispute?
- Does this company have a reputation for receiving many employee complaints or even lawsuits?
- Is the CEO just about to resign?
- Is management trying to delay a layoff that appears to be inevitable?
- How does the public view this company—as a philanthropic community hero or as a greed-driven monster?

All of these things have a great deal to do with both your short-term satisfaction and long-term stability at a company. How do you find out about these things? My favorite places are either on www.hoovers.com or at the reference desk of my friendly neighborhood library. Both sources are free, and both have more information on company stability, image and "culture" than you can imagine.

Let's pick a medium-sized hypothetical company from hoovers.com. We enter the company name, and we are immediately greeted by a great deal of useful information, including the following:

- The location of company headquarters and subsidiaries
- The names of executives and vice presidents
- The names and information of the company's main competitors
- The scope of the company's products and services
- A brief history of the company
- Some views on its further development

- Its ranking on a number of financial and business lists, including the Fortune 500 list.
- Archived press releases sent out by the company as well as recent (even same day) media reports on the corporation

Can you imagine an employer asking you, *"What do you know about our company?"* and your responding with the following statement:

> Well, I know you were founded in 1977 in Boston, Massachusetts, by Steven Gibbs, and that your current CEO is Karen Solomon. I believe that you first started with the production of only televisions and radios, but today the company is currently number 702 in the Fortune 1000 and has expanded its product line to a very wide array of electronic products that includes a launch of a wireless telephone device next month. I know that you have been voted as one of the top 20 companies to work for, according to Forbes magazine, and that all of those things would make me very proud to be a part of your team.

A little research beforehand and you'll be in command of all this data! You'll sound like you've been researching all night. Not *only* is it flattering to the employer that you know so much about his or her company, but it also says a lot about you. One would imagine that a person with this much relevant information under his or her belt would not only be well prepared but also intelligent, persistent, diligent, proactive, and persuasive—just to name a few qualities. Tell me one employer who wouldn't want an employee like that!

Use Your Library Card as a Job Search Tool

If you prefer to search for books and periodicals at the library, go directly to the reference desk and tell the reference librarian exactly what you're trying to do. Reference librarians, in my experience, are even more valuable than a good career coach when it comes to guiding people to exactly the kind of information they are looking for at this stage. He or she will expertly guide you to databases of newspapers, reports, reference books, and other written material that you can peruse until you find the information that seems most critical to the interview.

In most libraries, you can also use a database with valuable information on more than 12 million U.S. companies and 1.3 million Canadian organizations called *Reference USA*. If you want to arm yourself with even *more* facts, check out *Dow Jones Interactive, Net Advantage, Dun and Bradstreet's Million Dollar Database, Edgar-Online, CareerJournal.com,* or the *Riches' Guide.* You can even log on to these storehouses of information at home if you have a library card and a personal identification number.

Initially, research will lower your anxiety level because you know with whom you're dealing.

Finally, spouting off facts and educated opinions about a company are some of the surest ways to win over an interviewer!

CHAPTER FIVE

Winding Up
Your Strategy

> *I am seeking. I am striving. I am in it with all of my heart.*
>
> —Vincent Van Gogh

I bet by this point you're ready to grab your briefcase and run to your next interview. That's great! And your enthusiasm will help you in interviews too, but before you dash off, there are a few small (but important!) matters to attend to—those extra touches that will make you feel totally prepared and give you the confidence to stride into your interview like a champion.

1. You need to assemble some references and recommendations. (Don't worry—they don't have to be from the Secretary of State or Donald Trump.)

2. Next, you need to prepare a neat and classy presentation packet. A presentation packet is a simple paper folder with one "pocket" on the inside of each flap where you'll place some essential documents needed in the interview, like letters of recommendation, a list of references, and an extra copy of your résumé. (It'll cost you about 69 cents!)

3. Finally, you need to be *absolutely sure* that come wind, rain, or fire, you get to the interview *on time*.

Recommendations

If you are like most professionals working today, you'll probably hold several jobs between now and the time you retire. In fact, according to statistics compiled by the U.S. Department of Labor, most adults will hold over five jobs in a lifetime.

People leave jobs for many reasons: a better offer, a less demanding commute, a desire to change industries or cities, a discovery that they'd like to pursue another interest or dream, a feeling they've reached a "dead end" for advancement, or a better personality fit with their boss or coworkers.

Often these transitions are smooth; on occasion they are difficult or acrimonious. But if at all possible, try to get a letter of recommendation *on company letterhead* from a supervisor, manager, officer, or executive of the company before you leave. Most bosses, even when the separation from the company may have been less than pleasant, are still willing to write you a letter of recommendation. Even if you were fired, an employer would rather give you a positive-sounding letter and bid you luck on your way out the door than have you feel so disgruntled that you may take some negative action toward the company like suing it, or going to the media with a distasteful story. Although it's unlikely you'll receive a letter under these circumstances, a recommendation on company letterhead can help you enormously.

There are three sources of information a prospective employer can use to judge the character of a job applicant:

1. What the applicant says himself or herself, either in the résumé or the interview

2. What others say about the applicant in letters of recommendation and references

3. The applicant's own actions, which is an area an employer will know the least about until an applicant is actually hired

Naturally, the employer wants to know as much information as possible about you before making an investment in hiring you. A new hire, no matter how adept he or she is, usually means an initial loss of money for an employer while the person is being trained and getting "up to speed." It's usually months before the new employer starts to make his or her return on the investment in hiring someone.

If you don't feel comfortable asking your immediate supervisor for a letter, try approaching someone above that person, or someone even closer to the top. A letter from a coworker can also speak well for your character.

A letter of recommendation can be fairly generic (and you can use it to apply for multiple jobs) and would look like the sample letter on the following page.

If your employer is writing a letter of recommendation for you and is wondering what to include, tell him or her to outline the following:

1. Some of your most valuable skills

2. A few of your personal traits

3. Any of your outstanding accomplishments or contributions to the company

June 30, 20xx

To whom it may concern:

Jared Goldberg worked as a quality assurance director under my supervision at the Caliber Corporation from 1997 to the present. Under Mr. Goldberg's able leadership, the QA department designed and built a new database to track defective parts. I can directly attribute to Mr. Goldberg's efforts a 12 percent decrease in defective materials.

Mr. Goldberg is a trustworthy, intelligent, and professional manager in every way. He was responsible for bringing many improvements to our department as well as for instituting programs to train new employees.

In 20xx, his peers voted him the Caliber Manager of the Year Award. In addition to this, Mr. Goldberg volunteered his time in the Caliber mentoring program, and he was able to mentor six junior employees in the short time that he was with us.

We are sorry to lose Mr. Goldberg, but we recommend him unreservedly to any future employer. Please feel free to contact me at any time regarding Mr. Goldberg, and I will be happy to speak with you.

Sincerely,

Kelly Jones
Vice President of Operations
(222) 000-2276 ext. 45
k_jones@123company.com

Sample Letter of Recommendation

4. Things you may have done as a volunteer
5. Any awards or special recognition you were given
6. A sentiment that the company regrets to see you go
7. A statement that recommends you to future employers
8. An offer that he or she may be contacted in the future regarding your time at the company

Often, the manager or supervisor at your current company is willing to write you a recommendation . . . but he is so busy that it's difficult for him to finish the task. Ask if you can write your *own* letter of recommendation and have him edit and sign it.

If you can, include letters of recommendation from three different people, along with a fresh copy of your résumé, when you go to the interview. Do *not* send these letters to the employer before the interview unless you're explicitly asked to do so. Employers have only 7 to 90 seconds to spend reading materials you send before the interview. Don't overburden them with letters at this point. Since letters of recommendation are optional, and for "average" interviewers, rather rare, why not save the letters for a surprise bonus at the interview just to tip those scales even further in your direction when the time comes?

Be sure that the people who signed or wrote these letters know that you are applying for new positions so that they will be prepared if a prospective employer calls them. We don't want the busy people who supported you with a letter to say "Ellen *who?*" when it comes time for a prospective employer to check on your recommendations.

References

You need to prepare your references in the same way you prepared recommendations. Whereas recommendations are usually *written* communications, references are *verbal* recommendations. You do not need letters from these people. Pick them carefull, because employers really do take the time to check them! Any of your peers, and certainly your superiors at work, make fine references.

> *To get someone to act as a reference for you, I suggest asking very simply, "Would you feel comfortable acting as a reference for me?"*

If the person says yes, that's great. Tell her a little bit about the types of jobs you are aiming for, then write a thank-you note. Send your résumé with it. Sometimes when you ask someone to act as a reference, she says no. This can happen for a number of reasons; most likely, she will tell you she "doesn't know your work well enough." Don't insist—move along to your next prospect. The first person probably wouldn't have given you a particularly good reference anyway.

Bear in mind that many companies, especially large corporations, do not allow managers, supervisors, or any member of their staff to recommend an employee, either in written or verbal form. If it happens that you can't get verbal references or written recommendations from someone in your last company, try the company before that one. And then, the ones before those.

> *If you're having trouble arranging work-related references, other forms of references might be character references and academic references.*

You might also try the following:

- Ask someone you know who has a solid reputation in the community to act as a reference to your honesty, your integrity, and your dependability.

- Ask a former teacher or professor to write a letter about your ability to solve problems, learn quickly, and meet deadlines.

- Ask a member of a club, volunteer, or sports group to which you belong to attest to your skills and character.

Most people are glad to act as a reference and/or provide a recommendation—it makes them feel respected and important. They would genuinely like to be of help, and they would probably feel honored to be asked. Think about it—wouldn't you be flattered if someone used you as a reference? Just make sure each and every person you talk with also knows that you are beginning a job search and that a prospective employer at some point will most likely call him or her.

When preparing for an interview, you'll want to collect all the vital information about your three references together on one neat page. Type a document as shown in the following form.

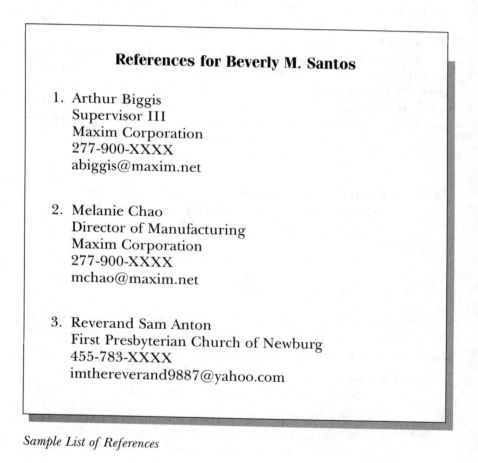

References for Beverly M. Santos

1. Arthur Biggis
   Supervisor III
   Maxim Corporation
   277-900-XXXX
   abiggis@maxim.net

2. Melanie Chao
   Director of Manufacturing
   Maxim Corporation
   277-900-XXXX
   mchao@maxim.net

3. Reverand Sam Anton
   First Presbyterian Church of Newburg
   455-783-XXXX
   imthereverand9887@yahoo.com

Sample List of References

The Presentation Packet

Now that you've collected your references and letters of recommendation, how will you organize them? Both of these items will be part of your presentation packet—something you'll bring to each and every interview.

A presentation packet is an 8½- by 11-inch folder with a pocket on the inside of each cover. It need not be expensive—just neat, clean, unstapled, and uncreased. The color doesn't matter. Make copies beforehand of everything inside because you'll be giving the packet and its contents away to the interviewer for him to keep and review. Your packet should contain the following:

1. *Left side.* Three letters of recommendation (not stapled). Place the most impressive one on top.
2. *Right side.* Your list of references (under the résumé—not stapled) and a fresh copy of your résumé (on top—staples are OK).

Present this packet to the interviewer after you've introduced yourself. Open it up so that the writing is facing in such a way that the interviewer can see it. Say, "I've brought an extra copy of my résumé and some other materials I thought might be of interest to you," and set it down with both hands in front of the interviewer. He may choose to read it later, or he may leaf through it right away and comment on it. Give the interviewer time to read it by not talking until he looks up at you and asks you a question or makes a comment.

Punctuality

There is one last aspect of interview preparation that we need to discuss before moving on to the second part of this book, in which we'll walk through the interview process step by step. It's about punctuality. Unless you know the exact route and the amount of traffic likely to occur at the time of day your interview has been scheduled for, it's a very good idea to make a dry run of your trip to the interview site a couple of days before your scheduled interview.

Take some time a day or two before the interview to locate the best route to the building. Don't forget to also identify the most convenient parking, and find out which entrance to the building you'll be using. Use the number of minutes it takes you to get to the interviewer's office on your dry run and *add* an extra half hour to it to allow for any unforeseen difficulties. Knowing exactly where you are going, how long it will take, and where to park will put you at ease and really let you know you're completely prepared for a knockout interview!

The Preinterview Checklist

☐ Do you have at least 20 to 25 skills in your skills matrix that you're good at and that you love to do?

☐ Do you have at least 20 to 40 Q statements that prove you can get results?

☐ Have you gathered your letters of recommendation and called your references?

☐ Can you answer the question, "What do you know about this company?" when the time comes?

☐ Are you absolutely committed to being on time and to doing the necessary preparation to be sure that you are?

Okay. If you feel strong on those points, let's move on to talking about the interview itself!

CHAPTER SIX

Managing the First Twenty Seconds of the Interview

> *The world is like a mirror; frown at it, and it frowns at you.*
>   *Smile, and it smiles too.*
>
> —Herbert Samuels

You have 20 seconds or less to impress upon an employer whether or not she should *consider* hiring you. From the moment you walk into her office to the moment you sit down in a chair, thousands of neurons will be firing in the interviewer's brain asking one of two things: "Is this person friend or foe?" It's an inescapable reflex, necessary to our survival as a species, to gauge immediately whether the stranger before us is going to help us or hurt us.

First Impressions

Whether it is morally right or wrong to judge a person the moment we meet her, it is a biological necessity that we do so. As long as we know that's a fact, we need to ensure that we use it to our advantage.

> **If you want the interviewer's initial response to be "this is a friend" rather than the opposite, you should follow a few seemingly simple instructions.**

1. Wear a smile, no matter how you feel. A smile conveys confidence, high self-esteem, competence, warmth, and enthusiasm. Plus, believe it or not, medical testing of brain activity has shown that when people smile, they actually perform better at what they are doing because they are using *more* of both the left and right sides of the brain!

2. Wear clothes that are appropriate to the occasion. It is not so much the color of your suit or the pattern on your tie that matters. It is the respect you show to the interviewer by indicating, indirectly, that the interview is an important occasion to you and that you value the interviewer's time so much that you have put serious consideration into your appearance.

3. Have a firm handshake, using the whole hand. A handshake that is too loose unconsciously communicates to the interviewer that you are not fully committed. On

the other hand, a bone-crushing handshake sends a message that you may be overly competitive. Neither of these messages is attractive to an interviewer. A handshake that is firm with one, two, or three "pumps" of the elbow is an appropriate business greeting, signaling to the employer, "Let's get down to business."

4. Address the interviewer as Ms. or Mr. _____ until you're invited to call him or her by a first name. Again, this greeting is part of being respectful of the interviewer's time and authority.

5. Introduce yourself by your first and last names and say that you are happy to be there. Do you know that only 40 percent of interviewers are trained to do the job of interviewing? My surveys of managers and directors from Fortune 500 companies indicate that they very often feel *more* nervous about interviewing you than you feel about the interview! Introducing yourself and expressing that you're glad to be there is the first step to putting *the interviewer* at ease, so that you can both enjoy a relaxed meeting.

6. Do *not* sit down until the interviewer suggests that you do. If he or she doesn't, ask politely if you may sit down. As soon as you sit down in a chair in the interviewer's office, you become part of his or her territory. It is therefore wise to wait until you are invited to sit or you have asked permission to do so.

7. Do *not*, at any time during the interview, put *anything* on the interviewer's desk. Keep briefcases, note pads, date books, and purses by your side or on your lap. The employer's desk is even more sacred and private territory than the surrounding office. Keep hands, elbows, and any other items from the top of the desk. If, however, you have been invited to sit at a conference table or a round table that is not a desk, you should feel free to take notes on the tabletop as the meeting goes on. These spaces are shared territory, unlike a person's desk, which is private.

8. Make your behavior in the waiting room impeccably professional and polite. Interviewers often ask their

receptionists what they thought about you. Many managers, directors, and executives rely on their assistants as a second pair of eyes, so you'll want them to give their bosses a good report.

Facial Expression

Let's talk about each of these steps and why they are a part of the almost choreographed ritual of getting down to the serious business of interviewing. First, the smile. You may take that for granted, but check your attitude some time and see how easily and warmly you can smile at a complete stranger. Practice smiling at strangers on the streets or from your car. Exercise those smile muscles so they'll be there when you need them.

A smile is not just another facial expression. *It's a signal to that primitive part of the brain* that makes the split-second assessment of friend or foe. It says, "I'm on your side. I will not harm you."

So, no matter how you may *really* feel that day of the interview, and no matter how silly it may seem to grin, *smile*. It will send a message to your *own* brain of being happy and at ease, and it will assure the interviewer's brain that you are there to aid, not to threaten.

Linguists and psychologists have said that 93 to 97 percent of communication is nonverbal, and the smile is one very important part of that communication.

What to Wear

Now that you're wearing that beautiful, warm smile, let's look at the rest of what you're wearing. Guess what? You don't necessarily have to go out and buy a $400 outfit to be dressed appropriately for an interview (unless you want to, of course). Maybe all you need to do is invest $5 in getting those dress slacks pressed or having that attractive blazer dry cleaned.

This is not a "dress-for-success" book. It's much more important that you look neat, clean, polished, and pressed. I'm not going to tell you what color or what shoes to wear. That's up to you. Let's keep it simple.

> *It is almost impossible to overdress for an interview unless you are wearing a tuxedo or a beaded evening gown.*

Dressing up is not only a way to make you attractive; it is one of the many signals of *respect* you will send to the interviewer during this first 20 seconds. It says, "I respect your time enough to think carefully about my wardrobe."

Many of my clients object to dressing up for an interview. They may complain that the vice president of the company is wearing shorts and sandals and has an untrimmed beard. Or that the CEO is wearing Gloria Vanderbilt jeans and cowboy boots. The difference between you and the interviewer is that you don't have an office with your name on the door (yet).

> *Before you get the job, take the time to be more formal and more conservative than you would normally be. (Then, when you're hired, you can don your army boots, expose your tattoos, and get down to work with the best of them!)*

Remember, it is not the price of your clothes or how well they match the latest fashion. What makes the difference is that you give the distinct appearance of having taken some time to put yourself together. A few guidelines to achieve that image follow.

Men

Shoes Hard-soled, hard-toed. The best colors are black or brown. No tennis shoes, sandals, or boots. I once heard that interviewers spend a lot of time looking at shoes! It would be a shame to go to the trouble of shaving and putting on your best black suit, only to find that the toes and heels of your shoes look scuffed and shabby. Take the time to have your shoes shined, or, if you're in the mood, do it yourself. It will help complete the picture for a knockout first impression!

Ties   Conservative: black, brown, navy, or red. A solid color or a simple pattern is best. Avoid ties that are too wide or too narrow. No potentially distracting artsy or modern patterns. No pastels or flashy colors. No bow ties.

Suits   Matching business suits are best. If you do not have a tailored, well-fitting business suit in gray, black, navy blue, or brown, you may, as a second choice, wear pants (other than jeans) with a shirt, tie, and complementary jacket.

Shirts   The only type of shirt that is acceptable for men at a job interview, in my opinion, is a button-down shirt with a collar. White or light blue, or a shirt with very narrow and light pin-stripes is best. T-shirts and turtlenecks are too casual, however tempting it may be to wear them.

Jewelry   Avoid wearing more than one ring per hand. Don't wear a pinky ring. If you happen to express your own style by wearing piercings on your lips, tongue, ears, or any other place that would be visible to the interviewer, I suggest that, just for now, you take them out. Wait until after you have the job offer and have put in a few weeks at the job. Then, you can decide whether piercings seem to be acceptable in your workplace.

Scents   Other than the soap from your shower and (preferably) unscented deodorant, do not wear any colognes or after-shaves. It's surprising what a strong reaction people have to scents! They either love them or hate them. Don't take the chance that you might be wearing the same cologne as her ex-husband!

Hair   Again, the rule of thumb is conservative. No matter what the length or style of your hair, it's worth investing a few bucks for a haircut before stepping into the competitive world of interviewing. Do not wear a hat.

If you have long hair, tie it back neatly, or consider, for now, having it cut. I'm not trying to tell you how to express your own personal sense of style. I am simply conveying what is true about hiring trends in the marketplace today. Interviewers prefer less rather than more hair on both your head and your face.

I had a client who had absolutely no job offers until he shaved off his shaggy beard. When he got a job (soon after shaving), he sure missed his beard, but he didn't complain about earning $80,000 a year!

Accessories   Always bring a pad of paper and a pen or pencil for taking notes. Avoid bringing a cell phone, pager, or hand-held device that may ring or sound off an alarm, which could send the whole meeting rather rudely off course. Even having a cell phone turned off and strapped to your belt, in my opinion, can make you appear to not be fully focused on the interview. Interviewers expect, and should get, your full and undivided attention.

By the way, whether or not you normally wear a wristwatch, wear one to the interview. It signals that you're conscious of time, and most interviewers want an employee who has that attribute.

Finally, I suggest that if you don't have a briefcase or masculine-looking leather portfolio, buy one. There are plenty of briefcases that look like real leather but are made from other materials and cost less than $25 at an office supply store. The same goes for portfolios. Maybe you have nothing better than a copy of the Sunday paper or the *Wall Street Journal* to put inside it. That's OK. Carrying a briefcase or handsome portfolio will make you look 100 percent prepared to do business!

Women

Shoes   Wear pumps with a medium-sized heel. Do not wear high, excessively spiky heels or boots. Black, brown, taupe, or navy is fine. Avoid flashy shoes with bright colors like red or glittery gold. No tennis shoes, open toes, or sandals. Flats may be OK for an extremely casual workplace, but low pumps are preferred.

Dresses or Suits   In the workshops I teach, I always have at least one woman who says, "I wore pants to the interview and I got the job!" That's good news, but she is the exception to the rule. It's fine if you wear pants to work if that fits the company culture, but an interview is another story.

I strongly suggest that you wear either a dress or woman's business suit. If you like, you may wear a skirt with a complementary jacket or blazer. Again, we're going for a conservative "business" look, so hems should be only slightly above the knee and necklines should not be revealing. The color of your jacket or blazer is not terribly important, but try to wear solid colors or very simple patterns so the interviewer's eyes are on your face rather than lost in the pattern of your clothing.

Of course, the most uncomfortable thing about wearing a dress or suit is dealing with those oh-so-fun pantyhose. Until scientists come up with a brand that doesn't run, you'd better be sure to bring an extra pair in your purse or briefcase just in case you get a snag on your car door or in the subway.

Jewelry Again, it's always better to err on the conservative side. Except for a wedding band and an engagement ring, stick to one ring per hand, one bracelet per wrist. Don't wear dangly or multiple earrings that may be distracting to the interviewer. Remove, just for now, any additional piercings you may have on your ears or face.

Hair and Makeup Keep it simple! Don't allow long or wavy hair to hide your face. Consider having a touch-up color, wave, or trim. Wear lighter or less makeup than usual. Do not apply too much foundation or eye makeup. If you use hair spray, you might consider an unscented brand. Any sort of perfumelike smell from hair spray, body lotions, cologne, or perfume can be disturbing to some interviewers.

Accessories Don't forget that your purse, briefcase, or portfolio needs to look good too. Remember to check them for scratches or tears, and remember to bring your business card. A pad and pencil to take notes shows that you're an attentive, interested listener.

These rules may seem stringent, but try to find ways to express your style as much as you can within these guidelines. Be sure to wear clothes you feel comfortable in and colors that compliment your skin tones. When you can look in the mirror and say, "Okay, I'm ready!" you'll know you've found a good combination of businesslike attire.

Your Handshake

By now, you're beaming with an ear-to-ear smile, and you look fabulous! The next signal to the employer is your handshake. In every seminar I give, I actually have the participants practice shaking hands, after which they give each other feedback.

Is it (like the story of Goldilocks and the three bears) too soft? Too hard? Or, just right? There is almost nothing worse than a noncommittal "dead-fish" handshake. We've all felt them, and there is just something intuitively unpleasant about them. On the other hand, the macho-rearrange-your-finger-bones handshake is not too appealing either. *Your handshake signals to the interviewer that you are about to do business.* If it feels, unconsciously, like a halfway committed or overly competitive handshake, you will not be getting off to the right start.

- A firm handshake, using the whole hand in the other person's hand, is an appropriate business handshake.
- There is no reason to shake a woman's hand any differently than you would shake a man's hand. Firm and businesslike is the rule to remember.

Many people, both men and women, have no idea how their handshake feels to other people. I strongly suggest that you practice it with a few friends or family members and ask for their honest feedback. Keep testing different strengths and positions until you and the other person feel comfortable.

Your Greeting

Okay, so I've asked you to grin at strangers and pump a few people's arms. What could possibly be next, you wonder? Riding a horse backward? Scaling the face of a mountain? Well, you're off the hook. Fortunately, those are not the skills you need to succeed at most interviews. The next four points are very easy and require no extracurricular practice:

1. Address the interviewer as Ms. or Mr., and introduce yourself by your first and last names. It will sound something like, "Hello, Mr. Isaacs. I'm Susan Sallinger. Thank

you for seeing me today." You'll be smiling warmly and offering a professional handshake at the same time. After the introduction, the interviewer will ask you to sit down. Don't sit down until he or she asks you to. If he or she does not ask, say, politely, "May I have a seat, please?"

2. If it's a small office or you are very close to his or her desk, you may feel tempted to put your notepad or some other article like a purse on the desk. *Don't.* The desk is the territory of the interviewer, and he or she will feel encroached upon if you pass that invisible line of his or her space and your space. Putting any item, including your hands or elbows on the desk will be taken as a sign of disrespect and an unconscious threat. If you wish to take notes, hold your notebook on your lap.

3. Don't take any beverages into the interviewer's office— spills or choking can be embarrassing and inconvenient. Even if you are offered coffee, it's quite all right to politely decline.

4. Turn your pager and cell phone off! If you forget and it happens to ring, do not glance to see who called. Simply apologize for the interruption and turn off the device.

Your Attitude

Have you ever noticed that when someone likes you, you tend to like him or her in return? Well, it's the same with interviewers. As I said earlier, many interviewers are going to be more nervous than you would imagine at this meeting. They want you to like them, just as you want them to like you.

It may seem hard to fabricate having affection for someone you hardly know or who doesn't seem particularly likeable, but there is a way. One way that I've suggested to my clients that really seems to work is that they picture the interviewer as a friend of theirs or someone they really admire.

You can pretend it's your sister Sylvia or your brother Harold, your Aunt June or Uncle Bob. It may seem a little bit silly, but I've actually told clients to picture the interviewer as a big stuffed teddy bear. Who doesn't like a teddy bear? In any case, your warmth will come through and will probably be returned.

Another thing to remember about your attitude is that *you* are interviewing the company, just as the company is interviewing you. When you keep that fact in mind, you'll remember to notice how you're being treated before, during, and after the interview. Do you like being treated that way?

If you were left waiting for an hour in the waiting room, if you were treated rudely by the receptionist, or if the interviewer was taking phone calls during your interview when he or she was supposed to be paying attention to you, you need to remember that you most likely will be treated in that same way on the job. Ask yourself the following questions:

- Do you like the general tone of the company?
- Do you feel respected?
- Do you feel you're being listened to?
- Are your questions and answers being taken seriously?

You might even think of it this way: You are hiring a new boss! Do you want to work for this person? Would you like to be around this person almost 40 hours a week? Would you like to be a part of this organization?

When you think about it, *the power belongs not only to the interviewer but also to you!* We will discuss more about the questions you need to ask yourself about accepting offers in Chapter 9.

You Passed the Test!

That's it! You've passed the audition! Congratulations! Now we're going to go for the rest of the play. The next chapters will give you all the tools you need to have a potent, masterful, and stress-free interview.

CHAPTER SEVEN

Answering Interview Questions

> Nothing splendid was ever achieved except by those who dared believe that something inside them was superior to circumstances.
>
> —Bruce Barton

All interview questions are not the same. Some require very specific answers. Some warrant more vague and open-ended answers. Still others do not and should not have to be answered at all. These more difficult questions require a special kind of strategy so that you can navigate around them. In the next few chapters we're going to talk about four types of questions and the special strategies required for handling each type:

1. Straightforward questions
2. Questions behind questions
3. Stress questions
4. Questions you ask the employer

We'll also talk about how to recognize and deal effectively with illegal questions. Finally, we'll review some of the most important facts about body language.

Straightforward Questions

Most of the questions in the interview will usually be straightforward. These questions are designed to assess whether you possess the kinds of skills, and to what degree you are in command of those skills, that the job requires. Your skills arsenal and Q statements should be able to help you answer almost all of these types of questions. Here are some examples of straightforward questions and recommended replies.

QUESTION: *Tell me about yourself.*

ANSWER: I have 7 years' experience as a case manager, specializing in issues of adolescent behavior, substance abuse, and juvenile delinquency. I earned a B.A. in psychology from the University of Wisconsin and a master's degree in social work from the University of Texas at Austin. In my last position at the Teen Discovery Center, I developed a curriculum to train juvenile offenders for job readiness. Within a year of the implementation of the program, over 75 percent of our clients found gainful employment and kept

Positioning Statement Template

I have more than _____ years of experience as a
_____ in the _____
_____ industry, specializing in _____,
_____, and_____.
I have an [A.A., B.A., M.S., certificate] in _____
from the University of _____
at _____ and an [MBA, Ph.D.] from the
University of _____ at _____.
I have also taken (graduate, postdoctoral, vocational, adult
education, internship) classes in _____
and _____. An accomplishment I'm
particularly proud of is [write a very strong Q statement that
fits the needs of the company]: _____
_____
_____
_____ I've come here to talk to you about
a position as a _____, and I'd like to
bring the same or better level of success to my work with you.

Positioning Statement Template with Fill-In Blanks

Positioning Statement Template

I have more than *10* years of experience as an *events planner* in the *high-tech* industry, specializing in *trade shows, international travel arrangements,* and *fund raising.* I have a *B.A. in business administration from the University of Georgia at Atlanta,* and I have earned a *certificate in international marketing at Simms Valley College.* One of the accomplishments I'm most proud of is *hosting a dinner with our CEO and the Georgia state governor. 110 administrators and government officials attended the dinner, and it ran absolutely seamlessly. I not only was able to complete the event under budget but I also received a handwritten thank-you letter from our CEO. Saving money on important events* is just what I'd like to do for your company.

Positioning Statement Template with Hypothetical Answers

their jobs for at least 1 year. I'm applying here today as a licensed clinical social worker because I'd like to prove we can get similar results with your clients.

Your Positioning Statement: "Tell Me about Yourself"

The question "Tell me about yourself" is most often the first question to be posed in an interview.

Although it may be interpreted as a personal question that requires a personal answer, it is really an opportunity for you to introduce some of your most important employment-related skills as well as your education and accomplishments to the interviewer. Your response to "Tell me about yourself" should be a very brief synopsis, or "sound byte," about your background.

Your answer to this question is very important because it positions you for the rest of the interview. That's why some career coaches call this statement a *positioning statement*. I have found an excellent formula for positioning statements that fits for just about every type of job and every type of industry. The template is reproduced here so that you can fill in the blanks. A template filled in with hypothetical answers follows.

I don't usually recommend that my clients memorize any answers to interview questions . . . *except* **this** *one*.

Your positioning statement is extremely valuable. It can be used not just in an interview but in certain social situations, on the phone, or any time you have the opportunity to introduce yourself to someone who could hire you or who knows someone who could hire you. It's good always to have this statement ready when you're in a career transition. I suggest that you work with the template carefully so that you construct something that's comfortable to say and that really feels like a good fit for you.

Other Common Straightforward Questions

For other straightforward questions, you'll want to use your skills lists and Q statements that you prepared earlier in the book. For example, looking back at your skills arsenal:

1. Do you remember your general skills list by heart so that you can recall them in the interview?
2. Do you have a good command over your personal traits list so that you can supply examples of them to the interviewer?
3. Do you remember your list of three competencies, and do you have anecdotes to support them all?
4. Finally, do your Q statements really paint a clear picture of what you did, whom you did it for, where you did it, and, most important, the results you achieved? If so, great!

If your memory of your Q statement and skills lists are not quite up to par, now is the time to go back and review them or make changes so that you have plenty of information to *demonstrate* to the interviewer that you are his or her top choice.

Here are some examples:

QUESTION: *What are some of your strengths?*

ANSWER: My strengths are my negotiating, training, and marketing skills. An example of my training ability is a project for which I trained a group of 16 new employees for the help desk, and they were able to function 20 percent faster than their predecessors.

To answer the question above, this interviewee:

- *Cited three* of her top skills from her skills arsenal
- *Elaborated on one* of them with a Q statement

Let's look at a different question of this type:

QUESTION: *What would your last boss say about you?*

ANSWER: I believe she would say I'm innovative, dependable, and professional. An example of my ability to innovate is that I wrote an award-winning software program for training new employees.

This time, the interviewee:

- *Selected three* top personal traits from his skills arsenal
- *Elaborated on one qualitative example* of the results of his work.

The same strategy applies for the next question:

QUESTION: *What do you think your former coworkers would say about you?*

ANSWER: I think they would say that I'm friendly, efficient, and professional. An example of my friendliness is that I always make it a policy to take a coworker out to lunch sometime during his or her first week of employment. I know how it feels to be new and how much it is appreciated when another employee makes the effort to reach out. It's important to me to help my coworkers feel comfortable. I'd like to bring the same kind of friendliness to your customers.

Confused? After a few more examples, you'll get the hang of it:

QUESTION: *What accomplishments are you most proud of?*

ANSWER: I'm most proud of producing, writing, and directing my own documentary, of winning a citywide triathlon, and of producing a show for CBS television. When I produced a movie-of-the-week for CBS, I was able to cut 3 days out of the production schedule, saving the company over $650,000.

Again, the interviewee:

- *Picked three* accomplishments (one from his personal life)
- *Elaborated on one* of those accomplishments with a Q statement

QUESTION: *What kinds of skills do you have that would benefit this company?*

ANSWER: I believe that my management, budgeting, and purchasing skills would benefit the company. In my last company, I initiated a new procedure for purchasing materials that ended up in a 37 percent decrease in annual materials costs. That's what I'd like to do for your company.

- The phrase "That's what I'd like to do for your company" is very powerful and persuasive when it follows an impressive Q statement. Try it!

The next question is one that might apply to a person who is completely changing careers. The question is posed to assess whether she possesses the skills for the new career:

QUESTION: *What prepares you to move from being a public health educator to a book editor?*

ANSWER: Well, although I have not yet had professional experience in book editing, I have 7 years' experience in the writing, proofreading, and editing of public health education reports. I have written and edited at least 40 reports of more than 100 pages each and submitted them to the state of Florida Public Health Department for review. I was also commended twice for writing, editing, and proofreading grant applications for over $350,000, one of which was submitted to the state, and one to the federal government. In addition to editing at my last job, I took an adult education class in copyediting at Seminole College in Fairfield. I'd like to be able to make similar contributions to your company.

QUESTION: *Why should I hire you?*

ANSWER: If you want someone who is going to raise morale in the company, I believe I am the one. Under my leadership in my last company, not only did employee satisfaction increase from 1.7 to 4.9 on a scale of 1 to 5 in only 1 year, but also absenteeism decreased by over 51 percent. That's exactly what I'd like to do for your company.

If someone asks you why he or she should hire you, you *may* be tempted to say, "Because I am the best person for the job." *Don't.* Though you may be right, the interviewer can't judge that from an unsubstantiated opinion. Instead, you can win over the interviewer by pulling out one of your best Q statements and adding the tagline, "That's exactly what I'd like to do. . . ."

The person being asked the following question is applying for a sales engineer position in a pharmaceutical company:

QUESTION: *What can you contribute to this company?*

ANSWER: Well, I can contribute an excellent working knowledge of pharmaceutical products, superior presentation skills, and excellent postsales follow-up discipline. An example of my postsales follow-up procedure at my last company was that I always called my customers 3 days after the sale and made it a point to call every 2 months after that point to make sure they were satisfied. I was very happy that we earned over $2 million in repeat business from one major customer in the third quarter, due to my persistent follow-up efforts. I'd like to make the same kind of profits for this company.

Questions behind Questions

The whole secret to answering a question behind a question is to understand the real intent of the question. To do that, follow these steps:

1. Become aware that the question is not what it appears at face value.
2. Determine what the interviewer is *really* asking you.

3. Recognize the interviewer's real *fear or concern* behind the question.
4. Direct your answer *toward* the real concern behind the question.

Let's take a look at some of these types of questions. We'll examine six sets of questions and answers, and I'll explain the strategy used to answer each question. Try to guess which of the answers, (A, B, or C) is the favorable answer. After a few examples, I'm sure you too will be able to decipher the question behind the questions.

QUESTION: *What do you think you'll be doing 5 years from now?*

ANSWER A: I'd like to be the vice president of human resources in 5 years.

ANSWER B: I would really like to make just enough money here to be able to buy a plane ticket to Hawaii and pay my first and last month's rent.

ANSWER C: My goal is to grow and learn more as a professional.

Before we look at the preferred answer, let's take a look at what the question behind the question might be. What is the interviewer really aiming at? What is the real concern or fear behind the question?

In my experience, when the interviewer asks this question, he or she is really asking two things:

1. Are you going to stay at the company for a while so that the time it takes to orient and train you yields a return on our investment, or are you here just for a short stay?
2. If I hire you, are you going to try to take *my* job?

Saying you're staying just long enough to get some money and skip town violates fear 1.

Saying that you want to be vice president of human resources in 5 years may mean that you will have to step on the toes, or, worse, replace your interviewer on the way up the corporate ladder. This answer violates fear 2.

C is the preferred answer to this question. It is open ended and nonthreatening. It is also generic enough that you can say it without feeling that you are lying. Though you don't say you'd be committed to the company, you do say you're committed to your profession. *You also express enough ambition* ("growing and learning") to sound like you're hard working and success oriented but not interested in rocking anybody's boat.

Let's explore a few more questions in this category. Try to guess the recommended response to the following questions:

QUESTION: *Why did you apply for this job?*

ANSWER A: I was just looking through the newspaper, and I came across this one.

ANSWER B: I have been targeting my job search toward major companies in the software industry. I came across yours on the Internet and decided to research it a bit further. According to your Web site, you've introduced several new product lines in the past few years. I was impressed by your track record and wanted to find out more.

ANSWER C: I heard about it from a friend.

The question behind the question is "Did you just stumble upon our company, or did you put some thought and effort into making a choice to work with us? Have you done your homework?" Answer B would indicate that you had the most forethought. Being able to answer a question like this one is the payoff for the research you learned to do in Chapter 4.

The same sort of strategy can be used for the following question, in which the question behind the question is also "Did you do your homework?"

QUESTION: *What do you know about this company?*

ANSWER: Well, in my research I learned that your company headquarters are in Philadelphia and that you have grown from one small office to over 56 locations in the last 3 years. I also know that at first you were primarily a brokerage firm and that now you employ Certified Financial Planners to serve the full range of personal finances and retirement planning. I also read a testimonial from one of your clients in the *Des Moines Daily Reporter*, who said that she had switched to this company from another brokerage firm because she felt that the planners at your firm had integrity and put her needs before their own. That kind of integrity in a company really makes me want to be a part of it!

Many of my mature clients tell me that they are faced with other versions of the question behind a question.

QUESTION: *Don't you believe you may be overqualified for this job?*

The *real* fears behind this question are usually:

1. "Are you going to leave because you don't find the position challenging enough?"
2. "Are you going to be unhappy with the salary we offer and either demand more or leave for a more lucrative position?"

This response satisfies all of the hidden agenda behind the question:

ANSWER: After discussing the position with you and seeing the job description, I feel I have a good understanding about both the responsibilities of the job and the compensation. I feel comfortable with both, and I'm eager to work for your company.

QUESTION: *What have been your most favorite and least favorite jobs and why?*

ANSWER A: I suppose that my favorite job was my last job as a Web designer. I think that the reason I liked it so much was that it was so creative and I never stopped learning new software programs. I've really liked all of my jobs, but if I have to pick one that I liked the least, it would probably be the job I had in high school as a parking lot attendant. I liked meeting people when they passed by, but I can't really say it was my favorite job.

ANSWER B: I have really liked all of my jobs equally. I guess you could say all of them are my favorite jobs.

ANSWER C: I think my favorite job was bookkeeping because I got to work mostly on my own. My least favorite job was the one I had as a senior bookkeeper when my manager was always checking over my work and telling me what to do next.

Like many questions and with the hidden agenda, the question above would probably be asked to uncover a "negative." Choice B is not really directly answering the question and sounds a little wishy-washy. Answer C poses the most negative issues because it indicates that this employee had trouble working with his or her manager and probably doesn't like working on a team. Choice A is the preferred answer because it states two positive skills that the person has (creativity and liking to learn new things) and the negative (the job in the parking lot) is fairly innocuous.

One of the most difficult and most frequently asked questions is the following:

QUESTION: *Why did you leave your last job?*

The *real* fear behind this question is that you may have been fired or that you are just changing jobs on a whim, only for the money, or that you are a "job hopper."

Let's look at three alternatives for fielding that one:

ANSWER A: I became aware that there were some excellent new opportunities in the field of biotechnology. I really wanted to expand my professional growth by finding out more about them. This company, judging by your Web site, seems like it would have some interesting opportunities.

ANSWER B: I felt pretty bored at my last job, so I just wanted something more stimulating.

ANSWER C: My last boss and I really didn't see eye to eye. He wouldn't give me a raise no matter how many times I tried to get one.

I bet you already chose A. You're right! No matter what question you are asked about your last company, your last supervisor, or your former coworkers, the intent is usually to "dig up" something negative. Both B and C imply some sort of negative response to your last job.

> **Sharing ANY kind of negatives about a past employer is to be avoided at all costs, even if you feel that you were treated unfairly.**

What if you were laid off due to a downsizing or reorganization of your company? The three rules of thumb for explaining a lay-off are the following:

1. Don't blame yourself.
2. Don't blame or sound angry with the company.
3. End your statement about the situation on an upbeat note by saying that you are looking forward to a new position with new responsibilities.

Try these answers on for size. They do not get into negatives, and they indicate that you have a clean slate and wish to move on:

ANSWER: Due to a mass reorganization of my company, my entire department was eliminated. Now I'm looking forward to exploring new options for employment.

Or . . .

ANSWER: Due to serious financial problems, my company was forced to downsize. Unfortunately, my position was affected. Now I'm looking forward to exploring some new opportunities.

Or . . .

ANSWER: My company reduced its labor force to accommodate
            a major shift in business. My function in the compa-
            ny was moved to a site 1000 miles away, where I
            chose not to relocate. I'm eager to pursue other posi-
            tions in the local area.

If you were fired, you have *no* legal obligation to reveal it. Many
highly talented people get fired incidentally. It's nothing to be
ashamed of. At the same time, it's not something to talk about in
front of a prospective new employer.

Your ex-employer cannot legally release the information that you were fired or say anything negative *or* positive
about your performance, for that matter. The only information
an employer can legally reveal about an ex-employee is the
following:

1. His or her start date
2. His or her title at the time of leaving the company
3. His or her last day with the company

You now have a strategy for answering some of these questions in
an optimal way. Keep the interview like a first date—memorable,
fun, and not too heavy. Don't get into personal details that may
end up backfiring on you.

What-If Questions

Questions behind questions often come in the form of what-if
questions:

QUESTION: *What would you do if you discovered that another employee
            was stealing from the company?*

The real concern behind this question is not what you would do
if someone were stealing. It's more about loyalty and whether
you have good judgment. See if you can guess which of these
answers would be the best for this problem:

ANSWER A: I would tell my coworker that it's illegal to steal from the company.

ANSWER B: I would immediately tell my supervisor.

ANSWER C: I would probably tell my coworker that I had suspicions about his or her stealing and that I hoped he or she would return what was stolen. If I noticed that the stealing continued, I would have to bring it up with my supervisor.

Answers A and B both make sense. They are not necessarily the "wrong" answers. Answer C, however, is the most appropriate one because it shows that the interviewee would first attempt to solve the problem with the other employee on his or her own and then get management involved only if those strategies didn't work.

Companies generally prefer that employees try to work out their problems themselves. It shows good interpersonal skills to be able to bring up something negative with a coworker. Of course, if the problem can't be solved, it shows good judgment and loyalty to the company to broach the subject with a manager or supervisor.

You might expect to receive several questions in the what-if category. Usually what-ifs are hypothetical questions involving morality, ethics, and interpersonal relations. The interviewer is not looking for an exact answer as much as he or she is evaluating your judgment as good or poor. Consider the following hypothetical situations, and imagine how you might handle them, should the interviewer bring them up:

QUESTION: *What if you noticed a team member really slacking off? He is coming in late, taking long lunches, leaving early, or chatting on the phone when he is supposed to be helping the team meet its deadline?*

ANSWER: Well, I might say, "Hey, Harry, we really need your help here. This is an important project, and all of us need to work together to see it through. You've got the talents to help us make the deadline. I really rely on you as part of the team, and I think your involvement would help out everyone. I have a lot of respect for your ideas, and I think we really need your input." If Harry didn't show some change after our talk, I would probably have to bring it up with our supervisor.

QUESTION: *What if your boss continually gossips about one of your coworkers with you and wants you to join in on the derogatory comments?*

Your reaction to situation number 2 would probably depend a lot upon your relationship with your boss. If you know the boss well, you might be able to say:

ANSWER: I really don't feel comfortable talking about Sally in this way.

If you didn't know the boss very well, it might be risky to bring up your discomfort. In that case, you might just have to listen to the gossip but not participate by saying anything bad about Sally.

QUESTION: *What if you have an important personal engagement that involves several other people, has been planned well in advance, and also costs a considerable amount of money, but your boss needs you, just this once, at the last minute to help her close a $3 billion deal before midnight?*

This situation is probably the most common and the most difficult to deal with. Having to stay late at work when there are family or social obligations is something just about everyone has to face at one time or another. It's a tough situation because someone is bound to be disappointed no matter what you decide.

First, tell your boss about the importance of your social engagement, but also reassure her that you will do everything you can to help close the deal. You might offer to stay a little bit later and be late for your other appointment. You might also say something like "I would make myself available by cell phone all night until 1 a.m. if need be, and then be on call at my social event." If you are particularly invested in your job and perhaps up for promotion, you might just have to accept the consequences and decide to stay until midnight to help the boss out. Again, there is no universally right answer.

If you have a significant other, spouse, or family member, you might discuss beforehand what sort of choices will need to be made in this situation when work and home obligations conflict. That way, you'll know if you have the support of your family to stay at work late, or if it's absolutely essential to choose your family or friend first.

Now that you have mastered the question behind the question, you're over halfway through completing the entire interview with finesse, competence, and know-how.

There are only two more types of interview questions to consider: stress questions and questions you ask the prospective employer.

Stress Questions

Don't let stress questions stop you in your tracks. That's *exactly* what they're designed to do! The lighter you are on your feet, the better you'll do.

The object of a stress question is not to gain information from the *content* of your answer. Stress questions are designed to gain information about how you *behave* under stress. That's why they're called "stress questions"—the questions themselves are supposed to create stress.

Let's take a look at one of the "scariest" stress questions:

QUESTION: *What was your greatest failure?*

You certainly are not obligated to recall your real greatest failure in front of a complete stranger. And actually, interviewers don't expect you to. Instead, the interviewer is testing to see how you react under stress.

How do you beat it? First, take a deep breath and entertain one of these answers:

ANSWER: Perhaps my greatest failure was not going to college right after graduating from high school. Anyway, I waited until I got a few years of work under my belt and then I got a degree in physics, with highest honors. I guess it didn't turn out so badly.

Or . . .

ANSWER: Well, you know, I was entered in a tricounty triathlon, and I trained for over 6 months for the race. I even hired a personal trainer and radically altered my diet and weight-training program. When the day of the race came, I was totally prepared and "psyched up" to win. I was sure I could place in the top three, if not take home the blue ribbon. I did the race in less that 1 hour, 32 minutes, 7 seconds. I gave it my best shot, but I came in fourth.

Or . . .

ANSWER: Once I decided to plant an elaborate vegetable garden in my backyard. I went to the hardware store to buy all the tools and seeds. I also bought a book on how to grow a vegetable garden, and I even took a county parks and recreation course on how to grow your own food. I followed all the directions I had learned, and I planted six kinds of vegetables, but the only thing that ever came up were the tomatoes. I guess I'm really much more of a corporate executive than a gardener!

With responses like the ones above, you're pointing out "failures" that are little more than minor disappointments. You'll also notice that you're actually calling attention to some *good* qualities like diligence, persistence, willingness to try something new, or even excellence. This approach works well since this is only a stress question to test your reaction.

If you have good rapport with the interviewer and can see that he or she has a good sense of humor, you might give it a lighter touch:

ANSWER: I suppose my greatest failure was not being able to take those three strokes off my golf game. [laughs]

ANSWER: I think . . . not being able to make a perfect soufflé. [chuckles]

One stress question that you are most likely to get in almost every interview is the following:

QUESTION: *What is your greatest weakness?*

Do not tell your greatest weakness! How do you think it would sound to say, "I'm really a slob" or "I have 27 unpaid parking tickets" or, worse still, "I am always late for work and I usually leave early"? Let's take *those* weaknesses (which of course *you* don't have) and leave them outside the interviewer's door.

The best way to answer this question is to pick out a negative that you might really possess but that could also be seen as a positive. Here are some examples. See if any of these "weaknesses" apply to you. In the left column is the supposed *negative* weakness. The right column represents that weakness when it's *redirected into a positive*:

"Weakness"—Negative	"Weakness"—Positive
Workaholic	Works hard. Would be willing to work extra hours.
Perfectionist	Is detail oriented. Sets high standards for work.
Tries to be friends with *everyone*	Is a team player. Has good interpersonal skills. Warm.
Competitive	Sets goals. Strives to excel. Overcomes obstacles.

I know some of these sound absurd, but let's take a look how the *opposite* of a supposedly negative trait can be turned into an excellent response.

QUESTION: *What is your greatest weakness?*

ANSWER: Well, some people have told me I'm a bit of a workaholic, and I guess, in part, they're right. I just don't mind working an extra hour or two or taking some work home on a Saturday if there's a really important deadline for my department to meet. Meeting deadlines is essential in this business, and I am more than willing to do my part.

A word of warning, though: Many interviewers have heard this supposed weakness so many times that you might risk coming off as unoriginal if you use it. Here are two other possible answers to this question:

ANSWER: Some people have asked me why it is that I try so hard to get along with everyone. I just like to feel that we're all working in a team environment where people need to like and respect each other. I think that when a team really gets along well, they're also more productive.

ANSWER: I've been told a few times that I'm just too much of a perfectionist. Yes, it's true. I do make it a practice of checking my work at least once or twice to make sure that it's absolutely accurate. When working in a medical lab, I have to stay on top of every detail. If the cost of knowing tests have been done correctly takes a fraction of a minute more, that's a small price to pay when someone's life could depend on it.

Even if the preceding answers sound a little twisted, they are better than bringing up real issues like not being able to follow directions or having hostile relations with coworkers. If you bring up weaknesses of that nature, you are surely going to invite the interviewer to probe further into the problem.

Another thing to remember here is that *this is a stress question*. It's not designed to specifically gather information about weaknesses. It is designed to throw you off balance. With that in mind, all you have to do is answer calmly with perhaps a smile or a little chuckle, as if you are shrugging it off.

Sometimes stress questions are very bizarre and seem not to relate to the interview at all:

QUESTION: *Why is there fuzz on a tennis ball?*

Either of these answers, said with a smile, would be fine:

ANSWER: Good question.
ANSWER: That's certainly one to think about!

Other, fairly silly questions that are designed to make you think they are "deep" and to throw you off are:

QUESTION: *What's your favorite color, and why?*

QUESTION: *If you could have dinner with anyone, who would it be, and why?*

QUESTION: *What's your favorite animal, and why?*

My advice is just to answer such questions at face value. You don't have to decipher their meaning. Interviewers are not really trying to psychoanalyze you; they just want you to *think* they are. Give a straightforward, simple answer to these questions, and you'll do fine.

Two more questions that may come up are the following:

QUESTION: *Do you object to psychological tests?*

QUESTION: *Do you object to drug testing?*

If the interviewer asks you these questions, you can at least be assured that he or she is considering you as a serious candidate for the job. You really can't win with these questions, other than to say:

ANSWER: No, I don't object to testing of any kind.

If you do object to being tested, you might want to look for some other target companies that do not employ these practices.

In Chapter 10, you'll be able to read an entire interview, from start to finish, so you'll get an excellent idea of how stress questions (and their answers) fit into the larger scheme of things.

You'll also get a sense of the flow and rhythm of the entire conversation.

Technical Stress Questions

There is a particularly insidious variety of stress questions that is usually asked in technical engineering or scientific interviews but that could very well also be used in other fields including, but not limited to, the social sciences. *Technical stress questions*, as I call them, are not really questions. They're more like little assignments. Their purpose is to put the applicant under a good deal of pressure. They may arise in an interview with an individual or in a panel interview. Let's take a look at one scenario to see how such a question typically arises.

> Abdhur Khatik has a Ph.D. in biochemistry and is applying for a staff scientist's position in a biotechnology firm. Abdhur did well in his first interview with the vice president of the company, and he has been invited back for a group interview with three of his fellow scientists. They're about halfway through the interview when one of the interviewers says, "Mr. Khatik, would you be so kind as to go to the white board and draw a picture of a normal cell?"
>
> To Abdhur, this request seems ridiculous and simple-minded. Isn't it obvious that someone with a doctorate in biochemistry would know something so elementary as how to draw a cell? Nevertheless, he follows directions and deftly constructs a diagram of a healthy cell on the white board.
>
> "There, you have it," he says, and smiles.
>
> There is an uncomfortable silence in the room. One of the scientists sits back in her chair, hands folded over her chest, frowning. Another seems to look confused and is shaking his head back and forth. The third comments, with a distinct tone of disapproval, "You mean, that's *all*? Aren't you going to draw the rest of it?"
>
> In reality, the drawing is perfect. The job applicant knows it's right, but wonders why the other scientists don't seem to think so.
>
> "Why don't you take a few moments to finish it?" the woman says.

With what you now know about stress questions, which of the following do you think is the best response?

ANSWER A: [defensively] There's nothing wrong with that! Any eighth grader would know how to draw a simple normal cell! Perhaps you've forgotten that I have a Ph.D. in biochemistry and have been published over two dozen times, not to mention that I have lectured throughout the world on the topic of cell biology.

ANSWER B: [nervously] Oh . . .uh . . . I'm sorry. You mean you want me to change it? Sure, okay. I'm not really good at drawing. Maybe you can't tell it's a cell. I must have forgotten something. It really is a poor drawing. What a mess! Sorry, I'm sure it's not what you're looking for. Should I try it again?

ANSWER C: [calmly] That's the way a normal human cell looks to the best of my understanding.

You know by now that a stress question is designed to make you defensive, angry, nervous, or doubtful. The best way to deal with the stress question is to remain calm and answer it in the best way you know how. Therefore, C would be the optimum choice in this example.

Illegal Questions

Ninety-five percent of interviewers will not ask you illegal questions. But some—because of ignorance, inexperience, or uncharitable motives—may ask you indirectly or directly about your marital status, number of children, arrest record, physical or mental disabilities, race, religion, sexual preference, or ethnicity.

You have a legal right not to discuss these issues.

One of the best ways to get around the discomfort of these types of inquiries (other than getting up and walking out the door) is to respond as follows:

ANSWER A: Excuse me, but I'm not sure I understand. Could you please rephrase the question?

That alone will usually stop the interviewer in his or her tracks. If he or she asks again, you can say:

ANSWER A: I'm not sure how my marital status would have any bearing on my ability to carry out my job responsibilities. Could you please clarify that for me?

Or . . .

ANSWER A: Does my race have something to do with the job description? I don't think I understand the question.

As for disabilities, according to the Americans with Disabilities Act, the *only* way that it is legally feasible to ask a question about physical or mental disability is the following:

QUESTION: *Do you have any physical condition that would prevent you from doing this job?*

Your answer should be no, unless you really are aware of something that would prevent you from doing *that particular job*. You may have a bad back or a trick knee or suffer from depression or diabetes, but if it doesn't affect your job duties as described, you need not mention it. The rest is between you and your doctor. You are not obligated to reveal *any* disability that doesn't directly impair your job performance for a particular job you are seeking.

The question "Do you have a disability?" is illegal.

It may be answered by a simple no.

Questions to Ask the Employer

There comes a time, usually near the end of the interview, when the employer will ask you if you have any questions about the company or the position. However curious you feel, now is not the time to ask whether you get an assigned parking space or whether you get an office or a cubicle. Those are real concerns, but not at this point.

Now is the time to use your inquisitiveness to ask openended questions, gained from your research, that give you information while at the same time flattering the employer. The following is a list of some good questions to ask:

- What is the company's 5-year plan?
- What is the company's mission?
- Is the company culture more on the casual or more on the formal side?
- What would be the ideal candidate for this position?
- What is the typical management style?
- What would be some of my duties in the first year of employment?
- What are some of the new products, services, or improvements in the works for next year's production schedule?
- What do you [the interviewer] like most about working at the company?
- What are some of the organization's proudest moments or most unique accomplishments?
- What do you think I can personally do to drive this company to the competitive edge?

Much later, when you are in the negotiating phase, you can negotiate for a parking space. For now, keep your questions open and general.

Stalling and Accessing

In some cases, there may be a question for which you just cannot recall the answer.

You'd be surprised at how clever your brain is if you just give it a little time to process and access a response.

You might take a moment to put your hand to your chin and comment: "That's a really good question. Hmm . . . let me see. I haven't thought about that one lately." This stalling behavior is perfectly tolerated by the interviewer because you are letting him or her into your thinking process. And, after all, you *are* human, and so is he or she! Interviewers don't necessarily expect you to answer on a dime.

Some questions require a moment to reflect. As you use this time (rather than panicking), allow yourself to take a deep breath or two. It's also okay to allow your eyes to roam or glance down at the floor, at a window, or to a picture on the wall.

Extensive research in how our brains access information tells us that sometimes it is necessary to look to the side, up, down, or even "into space" for a moment in order to give the brain access to stored sensory cues. These cues help us construct what to say next. Ninety-nine percent of the time you can trust your brain to come up with an answer.

If you can't think of anything relevant to say at that moment, the following answer will keep you poised, while at the same time showing that you are willing to take initiative:

ANSWER: You know, that's such an interesting question. I think the answer deserves time for some research. Can I look into it this evening and call or send an e-mail with my answer first thing in the morning?

Handling Questions in Nontraditional Interviews

What if you have an interview over the phone? You may be using the same words to communicate your answers, but you will need to pay extra attention to how you communicate warmth and enthusiasm. Here are a few strategies to use when you want your phone interview to have the same impact as being face-to-face:

1. *Stand up while you're talking.* You will breathe more deeply, and your voice will sound fuller.
2. *Smile.* Yes, smile! Professional salespeople are trained to use this technique so that they actually sound friendly and cheerful (even if they're really not having a great

day). When you are smiling, an interviewer can "hear" your smile in your voice.

3. *Listen extra carefully.* Since you can't see the interviewer, be sure you understand what he or she is asking. It's okay to ask an interviewer to repeat the question or to say, "I understand that you are asking me _____. Is that correct?"

4. *Keep your answers less than 90 seconds long.* You won't be able to see any visual cues, so it's wise to keep answers to a reasonable length so as to not let the interviewer become distracted or bored.

5. *Vary the pitch or tone of your voice more than you normally would.* A slightly higher pitch will communicate excitement, agreement, or enthusiasm. A slightly lower pitch will relay that you are about to make a very important point. Let your tone go up and down a little bit more that normal. It will keep the interview from sounding stale, as well as keep you feeling enthusiastic and excited about what you're saying.

6. *If you like, you can put a little stuffed animal or picture of someone you love near the phone and look at it while you talk.* It will make you relax and feel like you're talking to a friend. It will also fill your voice with warmth. Remember, whether it's the supervisor or a CEO who is interviewing you, that person has feelings, just like you.

In fact, 60 percent of interviewers you will talk to have never been trained at all in interviewing. Hundreds of interviewers have confided in me that they actually feel nervous, incompetent, or stressed when conducting interviews.

A little warmth in your voice, generated by looking at something cuddly, funny, or someone you care about, can go a long way to soothing the "rattled" nerves of some interviewers, thereby making the whole tone of the interview more relaxed for you as well.

7. *Do not ever discuss salary on the phone.* It's quite likely that one of the first questions asked in a phone interview will be, "How much are you making now?" or "What are your salary expectations?" It's way too soon for you to reveal that kind of information. In fact, it could cost you tens of thousands a year in lost earnings! In Chapter 8 you will see why bringing up salary at such an early stage is not advisable. That chapter will also thoroughly discuss the techniques for politely and tactfully postponing salary talk until you have a firmer idea of where you stand with the company. Note, however, that if you're talking to a professional search firm, it is OK to discuss salary early on in the job search process. The recruiters at the search firm need to know your salary range in order to find an appropriate position for you.

Group Interviews

As if *one* interviewer isn't enough, you may be asked to speak to three or four interviewers at a time. This is called a group, or panel interview. The content of the interview and your answers will not be any different than they would be with a single interviewer, but your greeting, eye contact, and follow-up will change a little. Remember these three tips:

1. *When you enter the room, shake hands with each person in the group.* It's great if you can try beforehand to get everyone's name, but that's not always possible. You don't *have* to address each person by name, nor do you have to introduce yourself by first and last names to all of them. A handshake, with direct eye contact, a smile, and a simple "Hello" or "Good morning" will do.

2. *Make eye contact with everyone in the room.* The interviewers are going to ask you questions one at a time. It's good to make eye contact with the person who asked the question and the others who are listening. Be sure that you glance into the eyes of each interviewer at least for a second on every question, no matter which one of them asked a particular question.

3. *Write thank-you notes to all of the interviewers.* It's worth your time! If you don't know their names or titles, you can ask the main interviewer or his or her secretary.

Body Language

Now that you know more about how to answer interview questions, I'd like you to know a little secret about body language. The secret is this: If you are sitting back, comfortably resting on the back of your chair, your answers will not be *nearly* as believable as if you are *sitting with your whole body tilted slightly forward in your chair*. Sitting back in your chair sends a signal, unconsciously, to the interviewer that you are not that interested in what you're saying and maybe that you're even a laid back kind of person.

Leaning slightly forward—even if you're *not* that interested in the interview—sends a signal that you are energetic and enthusiastically involved in the discussion. Who would you prefer to talk with? Someone who exhibits little energy and interest, or someone who you believe is very interested and enthusiastic? Surely the person with energy and enthusiasm would win out. As discussed in a previous chapter, psychologists and linguists estimate that a full 93 to 97 percent of our communication is actually nonverbal, so before you say anything, pay attention to *how* you are saying it.

Some other body language tips to keep in mind during your interview are the following:

- Is your body open and free to move and gesture naturally? Or is it tight, with your shoulders hunched up and your arms folded in front of your chest? Of the two, an open posture is certainly preferable.

- Do you make good eye contact? Remember, good eye contact does not mean having a staring contest. It is fine to naturally look away from time to time.

- Are you sitting slightly forward in your chair, with an open posture and without any habitual movements (like twirling your hair around your finger or clenching your fists)? Once you get the posture right and eliminate any unnecessary habitual movements, you should feel free to gesture and move about as much or as little as is natural for you.

- Are you fidgeting or feeling unsure of where to place your hands while talking to an interviewer? Simply rest one hand on each of your legs, or fold them in your lap.

You will feel most relaxed and comfortable if you just allow yourself to enjoy expressing yourself as you would in any situation.

Just one more hint: Mirror your interviewer's rate and style of speech. If you match your rate of speech to the speed of the interviewer's speech, your interviewer will unconsciously feel more of a rapport with you. Most of the time you will not need to do this, but if you get a real fast talker or a real slow drawler, that person will tend to feel more comfortable with you if you are closer to his or her rate of speech. Practice this with a friend or with someone you meet, and see how this matching technique will help you to feel more at ease.

Before we move on to salary negotiation, let's make sure you've mastered the interviewing ingredients to get a top offer! Take a moment to test your readiness with this checklist. If you can check every box, you're an interviewing pro!

- ☐ I know that the best strategy for answering straightforward questions is to tell stories with *specifics* and to use Q statements to highlight my skills, personal traits, competencies, and accomplishments.

- ☐ I've done some research on the company so I know which of my attributes to emphasize during the interview.

- ☐ I can answer the question, "What do you know about our company?"

- ☐ I know that the strategy for answering a question behind a question is to figure out the *real fear or concern* behind the question and then to answer it in a way that puts the fear or concern to rest.

☐ I recognize stress questions, and I realize they're *intended* to be stressful. I therefore *remain calm* and answer them to the best of my ability.

☐ I know how to answer the question "What is your greatest weakness?"

☐ I am clear that I will never bring up anything negative about my former jobs or bosses, even if I am asked.

☐ Just in case an illegal question is asked, I know how to handle it.

☐ I'm aware that the way I sit in my chair can either make me look enthusiastic or disinterested. I adopt a posture that shows I'm fascinated *and* fascinating!

☐ I have a good idea of some of the questions I would like to ask the interviewer about the company when he or she says, "Do you have any questions?"

CHAPTER EIGHT

Negotiating Your Salary

If you have to support yourself, you had bloody well better find yourself some way that is going to be interesting.
—Katherine Hepburn

Congratulations! You've completed almost every piece of the puzzle. You have command of your job-specific skills, your general skills, your relevant personal traits, your competencies, and your gift, and you're ready to use specific examples to demonstrate them at the drop of a hat!

> **Already, you are in the top 15 percent of all candidates looking for a new job!**

In addition to that, you have realistic examples of your skills and competencies, and more than 20 Q statements to back you up. Not only do you know how to *strategically* answer the most common and some of the most difficult interview questions; you also know how to stay cool under even the most pressured of interview situations—the stress question.

Now that you're a pro, this chapter will make you a master! You're going to learn how all of your hard work in the last seven chapters will pay off. You're going to grasp the techniques for bargaining for a salary of up to 20 percent higher than you would have expected. You're going to master the techniques of open-door negotiating.

The Negotiating Challenge

Have you ever noticed that your friends are more likely to talk about the intimate details of their health or relationships than they are about how much money they make? Do you know how much money your cousin, your neighbor, or even your best friend makes? If so, you're probably in the minority. For some reason, people just don't seem to feel comfortable talking about how much money they earn. If it's "too much," they're afraid they might arouse jealousy. If it's "too little," they may be afraid others will look down on them. Most teenage children don't even know how much money their parents make, much less how their parents may have negotiated to get that amount of money.

You'll find that, in an interview situation, both you and the interviewer will have a tendency to get the salary discussion out of the way and clinch the deal as soon as possible. Unfortunately, nothing could be more detrimental to your ability to bargain with the employer for the salary you deserve.

In this chapter we're going to bring the issue of salary right out into the open. We're going to talk about several things that are important to understand before you negotiate:

- First we will talk about common fears of negotiating and some responses to those concerns.

- Next, we'll compare the stories of two negotiators, Thomas and Stephan, and exactly what choices enabled one of them to get $30,000 more in salary for the same job.

- Third, I'll present what I call the *four bargaining factors*. These are four things you need to do and/or decide *before* stepping up to the bargaining table.

- Next, we'll analyze the technique of *open-door negotiating*, the surest way to bargain for a higher salary and more comprehensive benefits.

- Finally, we'll observe blow-by-blow salary discussions of successful negotiators so that you can see the four bargaining factors and open-door negotiating techniques in action.

Common Fears about Negotiating

You might be hesitant to negotiate because of any one or all of the reasons listed below. Take an honest look at yourself now, before you go into an interview, to see if you are holding any of these ideas about earning money or negotiating a salary. Most people try to avoid salary negotiating. In fact, it's not at all unusual for people to dread this part of the interview.

Here's an opportunity to examine your objections and overcome them. The effort is worthwhile. After all, the few minutes or hours you spend talking about and settling upon your compensation package not only will bring you immediate rewards but also will set you up for *all of your future promotions and raises*.

The five most common objections to negotiating that I've heard are the following:

1. *I'm afraid if I ask for more, I'll jeopardize the job offer.* If the company really wants you for the job, you'll get the job regardless of whether you do or do not try to negotiate, so you might as well try.

2. *Negotiating is only for aggressive "wheeler-dealer" types.* Actually, negotiating involves very subtle communication. You don't have to yell or scream or flex your muscles. Thousands of shy and soft-spoken people negotiate for higher pay every day. In fact, it may actually help to lower the volume of your voice during a salary negotiation.

3. *I believe that when a company says it has reached its limit, the company really means it has no more to offer.* Do you believe it when a car dealer tells you he or she "just can't possibly go any lower" on a $28,000 car, even if he or she says it two or three times? What about when an interviewer says he or she "just can't go any higher" on your salary?

   Unless you're applying for a job within the government or academia, your *employer most likely has 15 to 20 percent more for you in the budget* than he or she will originally offer. The trick is that you have to ask for it and prove (with your Q statements) that you merit the additional funds.

4. *It embarrasses me that I might be seen as "greedy" if I ask for more money or try to bargain for better benefits.* Some of us (most, I think) desire financial security and a measure of wealth so that we can live the life we choose. Wanting to improve your lifestyle and the lives of your family, friends, and even those less fortunate is not greed. A desire for your parents to have security in their old age and your kids to get a good education is certainly not greed. It really is okay to make money, and a lot of it. It's even okay to drive a fancy red sports car!

5. *I don't believe that my skills merit more pay than average.* Go back to Chapters 2 and 3. Review your skills and accomplishments. Take a look at your list of Q statements or

even say them out loud or into a tape recorder. Look at all you know. Look at what you can do. *Look at who you are.* You didn't just pull this stuff out of thin air. You really did it! You deserve an exceptional reward for the value that you bring.

One Job, Two Different Salaries

Let's have a look at Thomas and Stephan, two men who approached the issue of salary discussions very differently and ended up with quite different results.

Thomas is a 34-year-old technical recruiter with 5 years' experience. He's been out of work for several months and is getting anxious about finding a job. He's already gone into debt after being laid off 3 months ago, and he'd really like to get an offer from today's interview. In the back of his mind, he knows he will accept any reasonable offer. Anything would be better than continuing to be unemployed.

Thomas figures he already knows about interviewing techniques because in his last job, he interviewed other people. When Thomas interviewed for this recruiting position in a staffing company, he walked away with an offer of $30,000 base salary plus commissions and a full benefits package.

Stephan has only 3 years' experience in technical recruiting and is 37 years old. He's done considerable research on interviewing techniques, salary negotiation, and the company he is interviewing with. Though his finances have gotten very tight during a period of 3 months of unemployment, he's willing to wait it out for the right job at the right salary. Stephan has an interview today at the same company that Thomas is interviewing with. Although he has less experience than Thomas, Stephan negotiates for a salary of $60,000 plus commissions with full benefits, a hiring bonus, several perks, stock options, and permission to telecommute from home two days out of the week.

What happened here?

How did Stephan, with 2 years' less experience command $30,000 more in salary, plus extensive benefits, perks, and stock options? The chart below examines some of the things Thomas and Stephan did differently.

Thomas	Stephan
1. He took the first thing offered to him.	1. He *practiced* the technique of *open-door negotiating* (which you'll learn).
2. He did not research the salary, so it came as a surprise to him.	2. He *researched* salary norms so knew what to expect.
3. He did not know his bottom-line salary.	3. He *knew* his bottom line.
4. He was afraid that negotiating would jeopardize the job offer.	4. He *planned* to bargain for 15–20% over the first offer.
5. He believed that he was worth roughly the current "market value."	5. He *believed,* and knew he could prove, that he was above "market value."
6. He figured that "full benefits" meant that the company was giving him all the benefits they had.	6. He *planned* to negotiate for more benefits and some perks.
7. He felt a strong urge to close the deal ASAP.	7. He *made a firm decision* he would wait for right offer.

The disparity between Thomas's salary and Stephan's is not an accident. Stephan consistently applied the techniques of open-door negotiating and knowledge of the four bargaining factors. Let's take a look at what they are.

The Four Bargaining Factors

Salary negotiations can be a very delicate matter. However, the more you know going in, the more influence you can exert when the time comes. Take the time to research your salary carefully and determine where you stand on these four bargaining points:

1. *Know* the relative worth for your position in the marketplace.

2. *Clarify* what qualifies you to make more than average and more than the employer's initial offer.

3. *Determine* your target salary and benefits.

4. *Forecast* how long you are willing to wait until the negotiation resolves in your favor.

I want to see you get every penny and every advantage that you deserve. To accomplish that, let's take a closer look at each bargaining factor.

1. Know the relative worth for your position in the marketplace. It is helpful—especially if you happen to be entering a new field, going from a very small to very large company, or making a significant geographic shift—to get a ballpark salary figure for a position. Do some research to determine what, statistically, is a low, mid, and high salary range for a particular position. At no point should you confuse this ballpark figure for the actual sum you'll settle for. You should use this only as a broad guideline.

There are a couple of quick and handy ways to estimate what a reasonable range for your position might be. One is the do-it-yourself method, and another is to let a professional salary service do the work. If you would like to research your salary range and your probable benefits yourself, I suggest these free Web sites and links on the Internet:

http://www.salary.com

http://www.salaryexpert.com

http://www.jobsmart.org

http://www.bls.gov/oco/

If you'd prefer to have a professional service research your salary for a fee, I would recommend these companies:

Pinpoint Salary Services, http://members.aol.com/payraises/pinpoint.html

Personal Salary Report, http://www.salary.com

2. Clarify what qualifies you to make *more* than average and *more* than the company's initial offer. Complete the qualifications worksheet at the end of this chapter. What added value do you bring to the employer? Read the job description (if there is one), and analyze how and why you, as compared to the "average" applicant, can add more to the bottom-line profits of the company. Use your skills assessments and Q statements to make your case.

Ask yourself the following:

- Can I help the company make money?
- How about saving money?
- Could my skills be used to help speed up production, decrease waste, add a valued service, or improve customer relations?
- Do I have stories illustrating that I perform consistently over quota?
- Could I act as a manager or executive who would handle bigger budgets, manage more effective teams, and provide measurably superior leadership?
- Can I prove that my organizational skills can save the company time?
- Can I demonstrate that my public relations or customer service skills could turn the company image around?
- Can I help save training time by being an independent, bright self-starter who learns quickly and doesn't mind jumping in head first?
- Do I have innovative ideas that could bring distinction, respect, and perhaps awards to the company?
- Can I prove, with examples, that I can get it done faster, better, cleaner, safer, more beautifully, or more accurately?

Acquaint yourself with what the average job expectations are, and then use Q statements to prove you can exceed them. If there's no job description, look up a typical job description for the position in the *Occupational Outlook Handbook*—a massive encyclopedia published by the U.S. Department of Labor that features not only job descriptions but also salary reports, job requirements, and future economic outlook for more than

6000 occupations. You can access the handbook online at http://www.bls.gov/oco/.

The basic premise of all of these bargaining factors is that you are not a position. In fact, what you bring to the table may be a lot more than what the company had in mind for the position. Since you've assessed your skills and constructed Q statements in the last chapters, you are more likely to be able to convince the employer that indeed you have more to offer the company in bottom-line profits than the average person they had in mind for the position.

At no time, especially during salary negotiations, do you want the employer to think of you as simply "filling a position." Rather, you need to be thought of as an individual with special talents who can help the employer solve problems and who can add value to the bottom-line profits of the company.

So few people actually do a thorough inventory of their abilities and are able to communicate them. I'm certain that after doing the exercises in the previous seven chapters, you'll be able to absolutely shine as that ideal candidate who brings extra value to the organization. With extra value comes a higher salary. Let's continue with the last two bargaining factors.

3. Determine your target salary and benefits. Your target salary should always be 15 to 20 percent more than what the employer initially offers. Learn to quickly multiply by 15 or 20 percent and add it to your salary figure on the spot if you need to. Distinguish between the benefits you absolutely need and those you want. (See page 139 for a list of benefits.)

4. Forecast how long you are willing to wait until the negotiation resolves in your favor. Some people feel they can wait only 10 minutes; others, wisely, know that it can actually take weeks before a compensation package is settled. You may need income at this very moment, but the longer you can afford to wait for circumstances to go your way, the greater advantage you will enjoy.

> *Is it worth it to you to spend a couple of hours planning your negotiations if it means earning $20,000 or even $40,000 more a year?*

Okay, once you have determined these bargaining factors and learned the techniques of open-door negotiating, having a conversation about your salary will be like a walk in the park.

Leticia's Story

One of my clients, Leticia, was terrified about negotiating, and she told me that she had spent more than an hour holding her ground and reiterating her value to the company until, Voilà! She managed to go from an initial offer of $37,500 with medical and dental benefits to $51,000 plus bonuses, medical, dental, and vision coverage—plus a 14-day paid vacation and tuition reimbursement.

Interestingly enough, the interviewer left the room several times and insisted she had gone to her boss and that her boss had gone to the vice president, and that they absolutely refused to budge. But, because Leticia knew how to perform above and beyond the functions listed in the job description, and she had examples to prove it, the company finally caved in, though not without a lot of "drama."

It may look, in the final hour, as though the employer is about to fall flat on the floor and die before handing you the top rate for your talents, but I haven't gotten a report of a serious casualty yet. Hold out!

Open-Door Negotiating

Remember Stephan, who doubled his offer and got an expanded benefits package? Like Leticia, he used the techniques of open-door negotiating. Open-door negotiating may not be what you usually think of when you think about striking a bargain with an employer. There's no threatening behavior, no fists on the desk, no high-pitched voices, and no tones of finality. In fact, it's important that before I explain what open-door negotiating *is*, I tell you what it is *not*.

What Open-Door Salary Negotiation Is Not

I'd like to debunk some commonly held myths by telling you what negotiating is not:

- It is not a cutthroat battle to the finish, where the winner finally gets what he or she wants and the loser storms out and slams the door.
- It is not a balancing of a scale, where the two parties meet right in the middle and neither really gets what he or she wants.

Rather than using the metaphor of a "battle to the finish" or a "balancing of the scales," I'd like you to think about negotiating in terms of an "open door." In open-door negotiating, there are no declarations of finality, no threats, and no settling for something mediocre just because it happens to be in the middle. There especially isn't a passive acceptance of the first offer you get just because you fear you might lose the job if you mention a higher figure. Open-door negotiating is about creating possibilities, carefully weighing those possibilities, and coming to a civilized agreement.

The Rules of Open-Door Negotiating

There are several rules to observe in the game of open-door negotiating if you want to play it well:

- Try to postpone the salary discussion until a job offer has been made or until you are in a second interview.
- Do not be the first one to mention an exact amount of money, no matter how many ways the interviewer tries to get you to inform him or her of what you earned or what you wish to earn in the future.
- Speak in terms of ranges of salary rather than using exact figures.
- Postpone saying no to an offer until you are sure you have all the information.
- Postpone saying yes to an offer until you are sure you have all the information.
- Postpone, postpone, postpone. There is no reason to rush a salary discussion, especially when that discussion could add 15 to 20 percent to your earnings. Be patient.

Finally, remember that *your base pay is not the only thing you're negotiating for.* You're actually negotiating for a full compensation package that may include a sign-on bonus, extra benefits and perks, and many other features we'll talk about later in this chapter. Let's move on to an actual blow-by-blow account of a salary negotiation.

The Salary Discussion

Here are some possible scenarios that illustrate the principles of open-door negotiating and the use of the four bargaining factors. This is the story of Alex, a computer hardware sales engineer:

QUESTION: *What are you making right now?*

ANSWER: I'm making as good or better than a person of my skills in this geographic area.

QUESTION: *Can you give me an exact number?*

ANSWER: Well, you know, it's very difficult to compare what someone in a small company like mine makes with what someone working in a large company like this one would make. Maybe you could tell me what salary range would be reasonable for a person with my skills in this company.

QUESTION: *Oh, anywhere from $30,000 to $60,000, plus commissions.*

ANSWER: [stands up, puts his hand out for a handshake] $60,000 sounds great. When can I start?

This may sound like it's all too simple, but it works. This is a very typical salary negotiation for many of my clients. The scenario can certainly unfold in a thousand different ways, but what looks like luck here isn't. It's skill. Let's see what happened and exactly how Alex managed to pull this one off:

1. He never mentioned the exact amount of money he made, even when asked twice.
2. He did say he was in the "mid to high range."

3. He thinks of a reason (for example, it is difficult to com-
    pare salaries in a small company with those of a large
    company). Other reasons could be the following:

    - A change of geographic area (for example, from
      Seattle to Atlanta)
    - A change of level of position (for example, from man-
      ager to director)
    - A change of industry (for example, from travel to
      telecommunications)
    - A change in the type of pay structure (for example,
      from commission to hourly wages or a salary)

After he establishes that a comparison can't be made, he *turns
the question back on the interviewer* by saying, "What salary range do
you think would be reasonable for a person with my skills?"
Notice he *still* doesn't ask for an exact number. An exact number
would partially "close the door." Alex crafts his responses so that
the door stays open.

Also, he does not ask for the salary range for the *position*. He
forces the interviewer to look at what he, as an individual, can
contribute. If he had not done this, he may have been offered
only $30,000 in base pay. In the space of a moment, he was able
to increase the offer by 50 percent. This is a very dramatic case,
but it really does happen in this way for many of my clients.

Now that we've analyzed Alex's conversation with the interviewer, lets look at a few examples of how other job candidates
have been able to receive optimum compensation. Here's a story
of Wu-lei, a marketing specialist:

QUESTION: *What are your salary expectations?*

ANSWER: Actually, moving from the semiconductor industry
          to the clothing industry, it's very hard for me to
          judge. Maybe you could let me know what sort of
          salary range would be expected for a person with my
          background.

QUESTION: *We could start you anywhere between $50,000 and
          $62,000.*

ANSWER: [stands up to shake hands] $62,000 would be fine. When can I start?

Let's imagine Wu-lei in another version of the story in which $62,000 was a lot lower than what she had expected.

- If she says, "That's not acceptable," she closes the door to any other possibilities.
- If she replies, "How about $68,000?" expecting the employer to counter halfway at about $65,500, she still may be cheating herself out of thousands of dollars a year.

Here are some ways Wu-lei can use open-door negotiating by *not* mentioning any exact figures. She can respond to the interviewer's proposed *range* in a number of ways:

ANSWER: [leans back in her chair for a moment, thinking, then leans forward with direct eye contact] To tell you the truth, I was expecting something *somewhat* higher.

Or . . .

ANSWER: (Leans back and then forward) I was actually *expecting* a substantially higher figure.

Or . . .

ANSWER: Thank you, but I'd be much *more inclined* to accept an offer closer to the seventies or eighties.

Or . . .

ANSWER: Hmm . . . I think I would find the offer more *attractive* if it were closer to $70,000.

Clients often ask me what to do if the interviewer absolutely insists that they reveal an exact dollar amount for their current salary. There's a method for handling that one too:

QUESTION: *We can't proceed unless you tell me an exact dollar amount of your current salary.*

ANSWER: My base salary is $78,350 a year, and that is one of the reasons I'm looking for another position. I would like to be making more.

Or . . .

ANSWER: My base salary is $78,350 a year with an excellent benefits package worth $12,000, so that puts my entire compensation package somewhere in the nineties.

If you're at a first interview and are reasonably sure of a second interview, or if you're being screened on the phone, you should not get into serious negotiations. The question "How much do you expect to earn here?" is just a screening question taking to get you in or out of the next interview. The best answer is sometimes "flexible," "open," or "negotiable."

Even if the interviewer mentions that the position pays an amount that isn't amenable to you, don't reject it in the first interview. You haven't even tried to negotiate yet!

> **Your objective in the first interview is to get to the second interview.**

Hang in there. You don't *have* to accept the figure that is mentioned. Simply say you'd be willing to "consider" it. By the second interview you'll have a lot more bargaining power. You know the company is very interested in you. You may be one of only two or three candidates. You may be their only candidate. You're in the seat of power.

Another client of mine, Gary, was offered what he considered to be an unacceptably low salary in the first interview. He continued with the interviewing process and made it to the second interview. Gary was able, after a 45-minute negotiation, to get the employer to raise his salary from $35,000 to $49,000.

Gary did it by continuing to stress his skills and using Q statements. He was sure to let the employer know of the value he could contribute to the company, and he made himself absolutely irresistible. Earning $14,000 in the space of a 45-minute negotiation is certainly time well spent!

Benefits and Your
Total Compensation Package

You don't have to end your salary negotiations with the salary discussion. You can negotiate for just about anything. Here are some obvious and not-so-obvious factors to be considered in your total compensation package:

- ☐ Relocation fees
- ☐ Sign-on bonus
- ☐ Life, disability, and accident insurances
- ☐ Medical, dental, vision, and counseling benefits
- ☐ Paid holidays
- ☐ Vacation days
- ☐ Health spa or gym membership
- ☐ Company car
- ☐ Mileage reimbursement
- ☐ Training and education reimbursement
- ☐ 401(k)
- ☐ Profit sharing
- ☐ Commission structure
- ☐ Bonuses
- ☐ Performance and salary review after 90 days
- ☐ Stock options
- ☐ Telecommuting (working from a computer at home)
- ☐ Flextime
- ☐ Child care reimbursement
- ☐ Company-sponsored discounts on goods and services
- ☐ Parking reimbursement
- ☐ Commuting reimbursement
- ☐ First or business class airfare
- ☐ Expense accounts and company credit cards

. . . and more.

Creative Negotiations

Pat is a client who negotiated her compensation package creatively when the company she applied to "wouldn't budge" on salary. She got them to agree on $80,000 a year (more than they initially offered), but she felt she needed to make a better deal with them to feel satisfied working there on the long term. She had a great idea on how to narrow the gap between what she wanted and what the company offered.

- She said she would be glad to accept $80,000 if she could work a 32-hour week. In effect, she increased her salary by $20,000 a year.
- Pat asked that her medical and other health benefits begin immediately rather than after 90 days. She got that too.
- She asked for tuition reimbursement for a master's degree program that would further her knowledge of her field. She got that benefit also, and it was a lifesaver at $330 per graduate unit (about $1000 per class).

Use the techniques of open-door negotiating, along with the rock-solid confidence you have built while assessing your skills, gifts and accomplishments. Take the risk! It will pay off. I leave you with a phrase I once heard in the movie *Desert Hearts*: "You can't win if you don't play the game."

CHAPTER NINE

Following Up: Juggling Multiple Offers

Let me tell you the secret that has led me to my goal: my strength lies solely in my tenacity.

—Louis Pasteur

Focus Letters

You're back from the interview. Easy, even exhilarating, wasn't it? Celebrate, but don't pop the champagne cork yet if your offer is still pending. We still have a little more strategizing to do together.

Now is the time to get out a pen and paper or boot up the computer. I bet you think I'm going to suggest that you write a thank-you note. Well, yes and no. Now is a time when you can *continue to ride the wave of positive persuasion* that you created at the interview.

The note we're going to write now is a different kind of note. I call it a *focus letter*. Its purpose is to leave no doubt in the employer's mind that you are the candidate to hire.

A focus letter includes a gesture of appreciation for the interviewer's time, but also, and more importantly, it imparts a meaningful message of your newfound perceptions of the company . . . and how your expertise is indispensable to solving the problems of their business. On the following page is an example of a focus letter from a marketing executive seeking a position as the senior vice president of marketing at a software corporation.

How to Compose a Focus Letter

1. Determine the problem the employer is attempting to address in hiring someone to fill the position you are applying for. Some examples of the types of problems addressed in hiring strategies are the following:
   - Increasing the speed of production
   - Getting a better return on investment
   - Improving efficiency
   - Raising employee morale
   - Becoming more organized
   - Attracting more customers
   - Selling more products or services
   - Decreasing waste
   - Ensuring safety
   - Improving public relations
   - Saving money and time

Ms. Bettina Simmons
Executive Vice President
Ionit, Incorporated
554 Second Avenue, Suite 237A
New York, NY 103XX

Dear Ms. Simmons:

What a pleasure it was to meet you after hearing so much about you from Carol Jones! I must say I was very flattered that you extended our meeting from the half hour we had planned to almost ninety minutes. I certainly appreciate your generosity in sharing your ideas about the company and acquainting me with Bob Delts and the others on the team.

Something in our exchange rang a bell for me, and I just thought I'd share it with you. You mentioned that Ionit would be opening an office soon in Minneapolis and that a senior vice president would be needed there for a time to get the January product launch off to a roaring start.

I didn't mention it at the interview, but I happen to have experience with the marketing of DTrek 5001 and similar software. I planned and executed a similar launch in my prior position at 4Tell, and I ended up saving the company almost a quarter of a million dollars by including a direct-mailing component in the project.

I believe that I have the wisdom gained from experience to be instrumental in the same kinds of substantial savings for Ionit and, if hired, I plan to present several scenarios that I think would be beneficial for the Minneapolis effort. I also am free to relocate there until the product is off to a healthy start in the Minneapolis market.

Again thank you for your time in the interview. If you have any questions I can answer or if you would like to see a sample proposal for my ideas for the Minneapolis project, I would be happy to oblige.

Regards,

Han Nguyen
(212) 883-XXXX
h_nguyenvp@juno.com

Sample Focus Letter

- Winning an award or distinction
- Earning a place as a leader in the industry
- Changing the company image
- Outsmarting the competition
- Inventing new products, ideas, and services
- Bettering the skills of employees and managers
- Providing healthier workplaces
- Complying with government regulations
- Accurately accounting for revenue, taxes, expenditures, personnel, or inventory
- Keeping current customers happy
- Encouraging word-of-mouth referrals
- Revamping existing products or services

2. Decide on one or more strategies, based on your proven skills or your Q statements, that illustrate to the interviewer that you could be instrumental in helping the company solve its problems and reach one or more of its goals.

The Format of Your Focus Letter

- *First paragraph.* Begin with a pleasant, but not too personal, greeting stating that you enjoyed the interview and/or appreciated the interviewer's time.
- *Second and possibly third paragraphs.* Introduce the problem and establish for the employer that you have solved similar problems in the past. Mention that, if hired, you would like to get to work on helping the employer reach his or her goals.
- *Final paragraph.* Close with polite thank you. You might also mention that you will be calling to follow up in 2 or 3 days.

Tips to Remember about Focus Letters

1. Always double and *triple* check the spelling of the person's name and job title.

2. Send the focus letter within 24 hours of the interview.
   - E-mail is great.
   - Mailing or faxing is also good.
   - Dropping it off at the employer's offices may be intrusive.

Follow-Up Calls

At the close of the interview, it's a good idea to arrange a callback time. Three days is usually enough time to check in with the employer. If it happens that you have to wait for a long time to be apprised of their decision, call back in another few days. Many people are afraid they are being too pushy by continuing to call back. They're concerned that they will scare the employer away.

Just the opposite may be true. I actually had one supervisor tell me that one of the reasons she hired me was that I called back six times in one month to check on the status of the job. Each time I called her, I asked if I could call again. She interpreted my continued phone calls not as "pushy" but as "enthusiastic." An employer is always drawn to a candidate who seriously wants to work for his or her company.

It's okay to call once or twice a week. Set the pace and *make sure the employer doesn't mind.* You'll be the one still plugging away while everyone else has given up! Guess who they'll hire when the time comes?

Multiple Offers

As I mentioned before, by this time you may have several offers. It is all right to let one employer know about another offer providing it is a bona fide offer. We call this *leveraging offers.* You may be able to influence an employer to make a quicker decision, or even to raise the monetary value of the offer, but all of this should be done in a very diplomatic way.

Make sure the employer you are dealing with knows you really want to work for his or her company and you are not just "playing games." When you have multiple offers, there are usually some pros and cons to each of them. . . . *How do you decide?*

You decide based on what makes you feel good! Our personal values, to the extent that they are fulfilled, are what make us feel happy and fulfilled. Have you ever given much thought to how you prioritize the values in your life? How about in your work? Money is certainly important for most of us, but is probably not the sole criterion on which most people's satisfaction at work is based. There are other things of value like recognition, intellectual stimulation, social contact, creativity, and even spiritual fulfillment. Take a moment now to assess some of your values, so that we can use them to help you decide exactly which job offer is the right one for you.

Values Assessment

Please rank the following values from 1 to 22, with **1** as the most important and **22** as the least important value.

____ Financial security	____ Variety
____ Aesthetics	____ Independence
____ Competition	____ Minimum stress
____ Great wealth	____ Flextime
____ Social contact	____ Short commute
____ Recognition	____ Minimum stimulation
____ Helping others	____ Challenge
____ Using my technical expertise	____ Mastery
____ Spiritual fulfillment	____ Leadership
____ Intellectual stimulation	____ Routine
____ Excitement	____ Opportunity for advancement

Now please pick your top 9 values and write them below.

1. _____

2. _____

3. _____

4. _____

5. _____

6. _____

7. _____

8. _____

9. _____

Good! Here's an example of what I would like you to do with the values you've chosen. Let's imagine we have a job seeker named Tanya. Imagine she is trying to choose between a very large company and a very small company in the computer industry. Her top values (in order of their importance) are the following:

1. Great wealth

2. Competition

3. Recognition

4. Intellectual stimulation

5. Variety

6. Excitement

7. Challenge

8. Independence

9. Using my technical expertise

Evaluating Offers

Using a chart like the one that follows, on which the left side represents the small company and the right side represents the big company, we're going to compare which situation would best meet Tanya's needs for the fulfillment of her top values. If a small company would *better* satisfy a particular value, we will list it on the left side. If a value would be better fulfilled in a large company, we'll note it on the right side.

Here's how Tanya's list looks when it's finished.

Small Company	**Large Company**
Recognition	Great wealth
Variety	Using my technical expertise
Independence	Intellectual stimulation
	Competition
	Excitement
	Challenge

Tanya might make the choice to go with the larger company because it fulfills most of her values. A person with a different set of values would have a completely different profile.

Let's say we're looking at the same companies but with a different person. Carlos is recovering from a heart attack, and his doctors have told him he *must* slow down. Carlos's top values are as follows:

1. Minimum stress
2. Minimum stimulation
3. Short commute
4. Mastery
5. Independence
6. Spiritual fulfillment
7. Financial security
8. Social contact
9. Flextime

In our comparative chart, his values line up this way:

Small Company	*Large Company*
Minimum stress	Short commute
Minimum stimulation	Mastery
Flextime	Financial security
Social contact	
Spiritual fulfillment	
Independence	

On the basis of the values fulfillment indicated by the chart above, Carlos may want to go with a smaller company.

How do *your* values line up, and what will *you* choose?

Before deciding on that offer, please take a look at the interviews in the next chapter. No matter what you're like and what type of job you're interviewing for, there's something for you!

CHAPTER TEN

Sample Interviews

> You don't get to choose how you're going to die. Or when. You can only decide how you're going to live.
>
> —Joan Baez

Now is the time to put together all you've learned into a complete interview conversation. This chapter contains three sample interviews. One with Jerry Aronson, a marketing manager, another with Sarah Auschansky, an information technology engineer, and the third with Kei Soto, a director of launch operations.

Jerry's and Sarah's interviews include only what the employer and interviewee are saying, and they have only a few notes, so that you can get the sense of how an entire interview might unfold, uninterrupted. The salary negotiations illustrate a fairly straightforward manner of negotiating, which you'll recognize from Chapter 8.

The third interview includes detailed notes about why the interviewee is using certain tactics, to help you remember the reasons as they were given in previous chapters of the book. It also contains a more detailed and comprehensive salary negotiation, illustrating the nuances of the actions Kei takes to gain an optimum salary in a more complex situation.

As you read the interviews, let yourself get a feel for the flow and rhythm of the entire question and answer process. Don't try to analyze them too much—you already know all of what's going to take place from reading the previous nine chapters of the book.

Now is a time to actually imagine *yourself* in the scenarios about to be presented.

Jerry Aronson,
Marketing Manager

It's 10:30 a.m. Jerry Aronson arrived at the Walton Corporation half an hour early. He found a parking spot in the area that he had scouted out the day before, and then he took a few moments in the car by himself.

He checked to see that he had all of the materials in his presentation package, and then he put it in his briefcase. He left his cell phone and pager in the car. He was feeling relaxed, excited, and confident.

He entered the building at about 10:50 a.m. and introduced himself politely to the receptionist at the front desk, using his full name and saying he had an 11 a.m. appointment with Elena

Gross, the marketing director. In a few minutes, a woman came out to greet him.

"Jerry?" she asked.

"Yes, Ms. Gross," he said. "My name is Jerry Aronson. Thank you for inviting me today."

"You're welcome," she said. They walked into a small conference room. Jerry stood until she asked him to be seated.

"I've brought a fresh copy of my résumé and some other materials if you'd like to see them," he said.

"I would. Thanks," she said.

He handed her the presentation package, being sure not to place anything else on the conference table. The first 20 seconds had passed, and he had done it! He was feeling at ease, calm, and confident.

"Tell me about yourself," Ms. Gross said.

Jerry took a deep breath. "I have more than 10 years of experience as a marketing manager, specializing in strategic planning, forecasting, and customer service. In my last position, I oversaw a help desk of 65 employees handling up to a thousand calls daily. I have a B.A. in marketing with honors. I'm currently pursuing an MBA with an emphasis in marketing at the University of Phoenix."

"OK," she said. "What do you consider to be your greatest strengths?"

"I have strengths in the areas of quality improvement, product development, and training. An example of my quality improvement ability is a project that I completed in which I merged several phone line divisions into one unit, resulting in a savings of over $266,000 for the company and 20 percent improved quality reports from customers."

"What would your last boss say about you?" Ms. Gross asked.

"I believe she would say I'm innovative, reliable, and proactive. One example of an innovation I made at my last company was revising the curriculum for the employee orientation and training programs. The employees finished their training 3 days faster, and their work proved to be 15 percent more efficient than that of their predecessors," Jerry said.

"Hmm . . . good. Tell me, Jerry, what is your greatest weakness?"

"Well, I guess you could say I'm somewhat of a perfectionist. Details and accuracy have always been important to me. For example, if I'm writing a report for my department head, I want to make extra sure that I have exactly the right numbers before passing it on. That saves her time, in the long run."

Ms. Gross smiled at him. "Just for fun, what's your favorite song?"

He laughed. "Oh, let's see . . . probably 'Don't Rain on My Parade,' by Barbra Streisand. It's so optimistic!"

"Jerry, why did you leave your last company?"

"Well, as you can see, I am relocating from New York to California. One reason for that is, obviously, this great weather out here. Also, as I mentioned I'm finishing up my degree with the University of Phoenix. Most of the classes are online, but we go to one seminar a month in California. I figured it would be more convenient and cost effective to finish the degree out here, then settle down and buy a home in California."

"You have some excellent qualifications, Jerry, but we're also considering a handful of other highly qualified candidates for the position. Tell me, why should I hire you rather than one of the other candidates?"

Jerry paused and took his time answering. "I think one of the most important reasons is my excellent track record with presentations. In particular, one of the recent presentations that I designed and delivered to an audience of European executives won my company a $4 billion contract. That's exactly the kind of contribution I'd like to make to your company."

"What do you see yourself doing 5 years from now?" Ms. Gross asked.

"Well, as I mentioned before, I am working on a master's degree. I don't want to stop there. I'd like to take many more professional development courses so that I stay abreast of developments in the field. I think in 5 years, I would just like to continue to grow and hone my skills as a marketing professional."

"Do you have any questions about this company?"

"Yes, as a matter of fact I do. I noticed in my research that, in the last 2 years, the company has moved from number 214 to number 97 on the Fortune 500 list. What do you attribute that to?"

"We have an incredible executive team at the helm now. In the last 3 or 4 years, we've really streamlined our product line and redefined our market niche. We're all very proud of the progress we've made." Ms. Gross took a moment to glance at Jerry's résumé and one of the letters of recommendation.

"Hmm . . . good recommendation. Jerry, what are your salary expectations?"

"Well, frankly, making the move from a smaller company in New York to this large corporation in Santa Clara, it's rather difficult to know what to expect. What do you think a reasonable salary range would be for a person of my skills in this part of the country?"

"Oh, I'd say we're just slightly higher than back east. I would say you would start anywhere from $92,000 to $120,000."

Jerry stood up and extended his hand to Ms. Gross. "$120,000 would be fine! When can I start?"

Sarah Auschansky, Information Technology Engineer

Sarah hopped onto the subway and mentally rehearsed the exact route she would walk to the office when she did her "practice run" the day before. She knew she should be at her stop in another 5 minutes and that it would take another 10 to walk to her destination. As she got off the subway and made her way down the street, Sarah actually began to look forward to the interview!

That morning, Sarah had felt at ease and totally prepared, with her skills arsenal in her mind and her Q statements at her fingertips. Before she got to her stop, she made sure she had her presentation package, and she turned off her cell phone and pager.

Wow! This is getting exciting, she thought as she walked toward the office.

She arrived at the office with about 15 minutes to spare. She waited outside until 10 minutes before her scheduled interview time, then made her way inside the building. On the twelfth floor, she politely greeted a secretary, who asked her to have a seat in the waiting room. "Mr. Gandy will be free in just a moment," the secretary said.

Sarah glanced through a magazine, enjoying the pictures, until the secretary came to escort her to the interviewer's office.

She smiled the moment she walked in the door, extended her hand for a handshake, and said, "Hello, Mr. Gandy. My name is Sarah Auschansky. Thank you for having me today."

"Would you like a cup of coffee?" he asked.

"No, I'm fine, but thank you." She waited for a moment. "May I sit down?"

"Of course, please do."

The first 20 seconds had just ticked away and Sarah was still smiling! She sat down, tilting her body slightly forward in the chair. She resisted the impulse to put her purse on his desk and instead, put it on the floor at her side. She placed a notepad on her lap.

The interviewer was shuffling through some papers on his desk. "Sorry. I think I must have lost the résumé you faxed to me. You don't happen to have another one, do you?"

"Yes, as a matter of fact, I do. Here's a fresh copy along with some letters of recommendation you might want to see." She handed him her presentation package.

He glanced the over the résumé for just a second. "Hmm . . . very thorough. Tell me," he said, "something that's *not* on your résumé."

"What my résumé *doesn't* say is that I'm incredibly persistent. I can troubleshoot Ethernet, token ring, LAN, WAN, and frame relay. I don't stop until the problem is solved and the job is done. Once, at my last job, the whole system went down right on the last day of the quarter. Some of the other networking people panicked. I just stayed flexible and tried several different tactics. I ended up getting the system up and running within 90 minutes."

"Good." Mr. Gandy quietly took a few minutes to look over the résumé more carefully. "Your résumé looks good. Tell me, what would you do if another employee told you he had stolen something expensive from the company?"

"I think that first I would have to confront him face to face and try to persuade him to return it. If he said no, then I would have to let him know I felt obligated to tell the boss if he didn't return it. If that didn't work, I would probably have to have a talk with my supervisor about it."

"What development applications do you know?"

"I'm adept at Fortran, C++, COBOL, and SQL. I also have experience with Visual Basic and object-oriented programming. I actually trained 10 of the other IT specialists in SQL."

"Why do you want this position?"

"From the job description I read on your Web site, I think it's an excellent match for my skills. I know that you specifically require an expertise in networking, and that's my strongest area. In addition to the skills I mentioned before, I'm also an expert at TCP/IP, protocols, routers, switchers, and AppleTalk."

"How soon are you available for work?"

"I'd like to give my present employer at least 2 weeks' notice. After that, I'd like to start work right away."

"What are you making at the company you work for now?"

"My salary is in the midrange for an IT engineer in this geographic area."

"Exactly how much is that?"

"In the high eighties."

"I need an exact number before we can move on."

"I'm making $86,700 a year, and that's one of the reasons I'm seeking a position with another company. I believe a person with my skills and expertise can command a substantially higher salary than that. As to the exact amount I'm looking for, it's negotiable at this point."

"Do you think you could accept something in the mid-nineties—say, $95,000 to $97,000?"

"A salary of $97,000 would be fine. Thank you." Sarah got up and shook Mr. Gandy's hand. "Can I see some literature on your benefits package please?"

"Sure. I have some of the information on file." He handed her a packet. Sarah was pleased with the compensation package, which included medical, dental, vision, paid holidays, paid vacation, a membership to a gym, tuition reimbursement, and stock options. "This looks very good to me," she said.

"Well then, congratulations! You're hired. Welcome aboard!"

Kei Soto,
Director of Launch Operations

Kei Soto arrived early at the restaurant, where he was scheduled for a 2 p.m. lunch interview with the chief executive officer of a company called Panatel. He had flown in from Austin, Texas, where he was the president of Soto Partners, a small consulting firm specializing in interactive communications. Kei had already passed one phone interview with the director of human resources, as well as a face-to-face interview in Houston with the executive vice president of marketing. Now it was his chance to shine. He believed that today, if all went well, the CEO would be making him an offer.

Kei had flown in the night before so that he would be rested for the interview. He had gotten up early, worked out, showered, and dressed in a navy suit with a red tie. He had had his hair trimmed and a shoe shine several days before, so he was looking crisp and professional. He climbed into his rental car, briefcase and presentation packet in hand, and drove to the appointed meeting place, arriving about a half hour early.

Kei was already seated at the table, but he had not yet ordered when the CEO arrived and introduced herself. Kei stood up to greet her and shake her hand.

"I'm Tina O'Connell," she said. "You must be Kei."

"Yes, Ms. O'Connell," Kei said. "I'm pleased to meet you."

"Please call me Tina. How was your flight?"

"Oh, a little bumpy over the Gulf, but otherwise, couldn't have been smoother, thanks."

"Would you like a cocktail or something from the bar?" she asked.

The waiter approached. "What can I start you off with this afternoon?"

"I'll have a glass of the Stonehouse Chardonnay," Tina said.

"Mineral water is fine with me, thank you," Kei responded.

[Kei knew that ordering alcohol—even over lunch when the interviewer is drinking—would not be appropriate for an interview situation. Kei waited until the CEO ordered first and then was careful to order nothing more expensive than her choice from the menu.]

"Well, I'm glad we have this time together," Tina offered. "I've heard good reports from both Nancy and Ari about your work. Even though our company is a multinational conglomerate, I still tend to think of it kind of like a family. I always personally interview every executive from the director level on up, so I'm glad you could make it out to Florida today."

"I like that philosophy," he replied. "As you may know, I came from a small but successful company where we were just like family. There's nothing like trust and teamwork to build a strong foundation for an organization."

[Kei purposely answered this way because he saw that words trust *and* teamwork *were prominent in the Panatel mission statement when he was researching the company Web site before the interview.]*

"Tell me what you know about Panatel and why you want to work with us," Tina said.

"Well, that's easy. With a rating of 12 in the Fortune 500 companies, I think Panatel is a household word. Frankly, I've always admired not only the innovativeness and durability of your products but the fact that you are so active in giving charitable donations to adult literacy and cancer research. I would be very proud to work for Panatel because I believe in the lasting power of its products, like the VoicePan 2000 and TelEase Release 201BV. I also appreciate that it shares profits with the community and people in need, like 'Ready, Go, Read' and The American Society for the Prevention of Breast Cancer."

[Kei also found these details by doing Internet and library research into news archives about the philanthropic efforts of the company.]

"I must say, I'm very impressed with how much you know about our company," Tina said.

"I guess I just really enjoy doing research," Kei responded. "I like to go into any endeavor with as much knowledge and information as I can so that I can analyze the situation before coming up with a plan of action. I'd really like to tell you about a project at my former company for which I spearheaded some research into a product launch in the previously untouched Latin American market. When we finally launched the voice recognition software into that market, we were able to report a return on investment within only 9 months, because of careful research and forecasting."

[Note that "research" was one of the critical key words in the job description. Kei carefully guided the conversation to one of his key accomplishments, even though he wasn't directly asked to do so.]

"Good. Kei, I understand you currently live in Texas. Will relocation be a problem for you?"

"Not in the least. I've already discussed the possibility of making a move with my family, so we've been expecting a change for quite a while. You see I have another offer pending from Nusite in Denver that would also require relocation. My wife, in fact, was quick to let me know that she'd prefer being here in Fort Lauderdale than in Denver. We have an extended family here in Florida, and since my wife completed her MBA at Florida State

University, she still has quite a few contacts here. We'd be happy to be closer to the family and friends. By the way, we're completely prepared to pay all relocation costs. I anticipate the move will be smooth, quick, and efficient."

[Kei recognized that the question "Will relocation be a problem for you?" was actually a question behind a question. The interviewer may be fishing for whether Kei would require expensive relocation fees. In this case, he anticipated her concern and quickly quelled it by saying that he was going to pay for relocation costs.]

Lunch arrived, and Kei was careful to wait to take his first bite until after Tina had taken hers.

"I know you were president of your own company. Does making a move to the director level seem like a step down to you?"

"Not at all. In fact, when I think of working for a company as prominent as Panatel, it seems to me to be more of a lateral move, considering that my company was relatively small and unknown. I've read the job description of director of launch operations, and it sounds like a very interesting challenge for me, something I would like to sink my teeth into over the long term. I'm also very aware of what might be the possible salary range for the position, and it sounds reasonable for me financially. I'd be very pleased to make a long-term commitment to work here as a director, and I think the position will pose some very interesting problems to solve, which is exactly what I love to do most."

[Again Kei recognized that the question behind a question about moving down in rank was really a question about whether he might be overqualified for the position and therefore unhappy with either the job description or the salary. He recognized the concern behind the question and addressed it immediately by saying he would be happy in the position and satisfied with the salary.]

"I'm wondering what sort of salary you're expecting."

Kei replied, "Moving from Texas to Fort Lauderdale and from a small company of my own to a major Fortune 500 company, it's rather difficult for me to come up with an exact number. Perhaps you could tell me a reasonable range for a person with my skills."

"What range did you have in mind?"

"Well," Kei replied, "for a person with more than 10 years' experience in marketing and an MBA, I consider myself a candidate for the mid to high range of a director's position in this geographic area.

"What exactly would that be?" Tina queried.

[Kei knew that the advertised range for the salary was between $129,000 and $146,000 a year. However, he calculated that the company would most likely have 15 to 20 percent more to offer him.]

"Well," he said, "I would say that starting at something above $165,000 would be reasonable."

"Kei, our salary range for this position is from $129,000 to $146,000, and I'm not sure we'll be able to go beyond that."

"Although $146,000 sounds like something I would consider, I would actually be more inclined to accept a substantially higher offer. Since I've led launches of over 20 products that have earned a return on investment in as quick as 9 months, I'm more than certain that I can bring Panatel this same aggressive approach to making immediate profits. If we can agree on a sum that's somewhat higher, it would ensure that I would find this offer more attractive than the one I've received at Nusite."

[Notice that Kei said he would "consider" $146,000. That indicated that he was interested in the position, but he didn't have to get stuck on that sum. He also kept the door open by not rejecting the offer at this early stage of negotiations.

You'll see that he strategically used the phrases "substantially higher" and "somewhat higher" to avoid mentioning an exact number. Phrases like "I'd be more inclined . . ." and "the offer would be more attractive . . ." also lend themselves to keeping options open and follow the guidelines of open-door negotiating.

Kei used the technique of "leveraging offers" when he alluded to (but does not go into detail about) the real offer he had from Nusite. He also reminded the CEO that he offers considerably more value than just "filling a position," by highlighting one of his more impressive past accomplishments, adding that he planned to use those same talents to add value to Panatel.]

Tina listened and agreed: "All right, I'm prepared to offer you closer to what you're asking for. Are you prepared to take a stab at finding a suitable number?"

"Thank you. I appreciate that. I think an appropriate salary for the contribution I plan to make would be something closer to the high $160,000 range."

[He got closer to a number here but still did not lock himself into an exact figure.]

"Then how about $169,000 to start?" she offered.

He quickly said, with a smile and hand extended for a hand-shake, "$171,000 and I'll sign on, providing the benefits are within my expectations."

"$171,000 it is," she agreed. "We're glad to have you on the team!" They shook hands over the table. "I'd like to have you meet with a human resources representative who handles benefits to discuss exactly what your total compensation package would be. I'll have my assistant arrange a meeting sometime tomorrow so we can bring the offer to a close. If everything is amenable to you, you should be receiving an offer letter by mail in 5 to 7 days."

Kei was delighted. "Thanks. I think we've had a productive meeting today, and thank you for lunch by the way. After meeting with human resources, I'd like to take 48 hours to evaluate the entire compensation package, review what we said today, and discuss the move with my wife so that I can officially accept the offer."

[He actually used this time to go back to Nusite with a counteroffer to the $165,000 they had originally offered, seeing if he could leverage the Panatel offer for an even higher salary at Nusite.]

"That'll be fine," said the CEO. "It looks like we'll be in business by the beginning of next month."

"Tina, I really appreciate the job offer, and I think that our agreement will be mutually beneficial and profitable. Thanks again for your time. It's been a pleasure to meet and talk with you." They shook hands. "Enjoy the rest of your day."

"Sure thing. Have a safe trip home. Good-bye."

Kei returned home after meeting with human resources and negotiating for medical; dental; vision; 401(k); and vacation, sick, and holiday time. He also received a membership to the local gym, first-class airfare for any business-related travel, a life insurance policy, and stock options.

To seal the deal, after Kei got back to Texas, he wrote a focus letter, reiterating his promise to seek a quick return on investments and thanking all the people who had interviewed him for their time. He and his wife decided that although Nusite raised their offer to $173,000, they would rather spend their time and retire in Florida than Colorado.

The official offer letter from Panatel arrived in the mail a few days later. Apparently, they had decided to offer him $12,000 in relocation fees after all, on top of everything else he'd negotiated for. He smiled and signed on the dotted line.

CHAPTER ELEVEN

Practice Questions

> *Perhaps I am stronger than I think!*
>
> —Thomas Merton

In the following practice section, feel free to refer to the book if you like. Chapters 2, 3, 7, and 8 will be most useful to you in this process. As you answer the questions, ask yourself, "What category of question is this, and what strategy do I need to answer it?"

Tell me about yourself.

_____

_____

_____

_____

_____

_____

_____

What are some of your strengths?

_____

_____

_____

_____

Tell me about some of your skills that apply to this job.

_____

_____

_____

_____

What accomplishment do you feel most proud of?

_____

_____

_____

_____

What would you do if you caught a coworker stealing?

_____

_____

_____

_____

What was your favorite class in school?

_____

_____

_____

_____

Tell me what you think your former coworkers would say about you.

_____

_____

_____

_____

What did you think about your former boss?

_____

_____

_____

_____

Why are you leaving your former company?

_____

_____

_____

_____

Why would you like to work for this company?

_____

_____

_____

_____

What do you see yourself doing 5 years from now?

_____

_____

_____

_____

Don't you think you might be too inexperienced/overquali-
fied for this position?

_____

_____

_____

_____

Do you have a disability?

_____

_____

_____

Why did you never finish your degree?

_____

_____

_____

What do you usually do on weekends?

_____

_____

_____

Just out of curiosity, what's your favorite color?

_____

_____

_____

What do you consider to be your greatest failure?

_____

_____

_____

What weaknesses do you think you have?

_____
_____
_____
_____

Have you ever been late for work or an important appointment?

_____
_____
_____
_____

How much do you know about our company?

_____
_____
_____
_____

Would you object to personality or drug testing?

_____
_____
_____
_____

How do you explain that you were at your last company for only 1 year/1 month?

_____
_____
_____
_____

What were you doing between the time you worked for that company and today?

_____
_____
_____
_____

What is the most difficult interpersonal situation you have had to deal with at work, and how did you handle it?

_____

_____

_____

_____

What do you expect to earn here?

_____

_____

_____

_____

What was your salary in your last position?

_____

_____

_____

_____

Are you looking for a position in many other companies?

_____

_____

_____

_____

Why do you think you deserve more than what we usually pay for this position?

_____

_____

_____

_____

Are you familiar with our company mission statement, and if so, what do you think of it?

_____

_____

_____

_____

How would you describe your personality?

_____

_____

_____

_____

When would you be willing to start work?

_____

_____

_____

_____

Give me an example of how you react to change.

_____

_____

_____

_____

What do you think you could accomplish in your first year here?

_____

_____

_____

_____

May we call your references?

_____

_____

_____

_____

We have many applicants for this position. Why should I hire you?

_____

_____

_____

_____

Confidence

> *To have that sense of one's intrinsic worth, which constitutes self-respect, is to potentially have everything.*
> —Joan Didion

I recently had a woman write to me after participating in a Fearless Interviewing seminar and tell me simply, that Fearless Interviewing had given her the confidence she needed to go through an interview. I thought carefully about the word *confidence* because so many people who've attended the seminars have also responded that it gave them just that. What is confidence?

The Latin translation of the word *confidence* means "with courage," "with faith," "with trust," and "without fear." You have actually done, through the exercises in this book, what few people have taken the time to do. You're not fumbling your way into an interview with blind faith and proclaiming, "I'm great! I'm the best! I need the job! Hire me!"

You're walking in holding your head high and wearing a smile on your face, knowing that you have a strategy for the entire meeting, from beginning, to middle, to end. It gives you a sense of rock-solid clarity to know your skills, know how to express them, and know how to persuade the employer to value them too. You know that your assertions are based on truth and that you need not be fooled by an interviewer's hidden agenda or a question designed to throw you off base. You know yourself, and you know that your pride in your accomplishments is not based on arrogance but on the palpable realization that by the effort of your own hands, heart, and mind, *you* have, in fact, achieved those things, however large or small.

At the beginning of this book, I told you that when you had progressed through a few basic steps, you'd be flying. Here you are, on the launching pad! (To those of you already beginning your flight, wait a minute: Can you stay in your chair for just a moment more?) I want to talk to you before you go out there and unleash yourself onto the world.

You are a precious, smart, and courageous human being. Unless you believe that we live in a cruel universe (which I don't), then this universe will provide for you an occupation—a way to spend your time and energy—and a livelihood, a way to make a living.

There is a rite of passage into that occupation. We call it an *interview*.

An interview is simply an opportunity for you to talk about what you enjoy doing most and what you do best. Yes, there are snares and traps along the way, just as there are in any journey worth taking, but you see, we've uncovered them all! You *know* where to look, you've *planned* where to step, and you've already taken this journey safely in your mind. You're there! Your spirit is filled with confidence.

Nothing can stop you.

INDEX

Index

ABOUT THE AUTHOR

Marky Stein is founder of a successful career-consulting firm. She is a popular speaker at professional and career development conferences and has written for *The Wall Street Journal* and other national publications. Ms. Stein has counseled groups and individuals from more than 40 of the Fortune 500 companies. She is also the online Job Search Expert at *iVillage.com*.